KU-274-940

ARE YOU READY FOR YOUR
Twisted Journeys®?

YOU ARE THE HERO OF THE BOOK
YOU'RE ABOUT TO READ. YOUR
JOURNEYS WILL BE PACKED WITH
ADVENTURES IN A WORLD OF
MAGIC AND MONSTERS.
AND EVERY STORY STARS **YOU!**

EACH PAGE TELLS WHAT HAPPENS TO **YOU**
AS YOU EXPLORE MOUNT FATE, SEARCH FOR
TREASURE AND FACE DANGERS YOU NEVER EXPECTED.
YOUR WORDS AND THOUGHTS ARE SHOWN IN THE **YELLOW
BALLOONS.** AND YOU GET TO DECIDE WHAT HAPPENS NEXT.
JUST FOLLOW THE NOTE AT THE BOTTOM OF EACH
PAGE UNTIL YOU REACH A *Twisted Journeys®* PAGE.
THEN MAKE THE CHOICE **YOU** LIKE BEST.

BUT BE CAREFUL...THE WRONG CHOICE
COULD MAKE YOUR ADVENTURING
DAYS VERY SHORT!

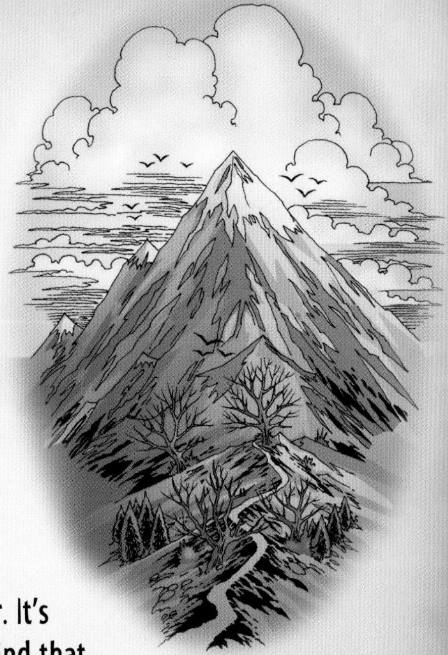

Above you loom the crags of Mount Fate. The early autumn sun glints off the snow that lines the peak. You push back the guard on your helm and take in the sight.

You dismount from your horse and slide your sword back into the scabbard on your back. You see your breath whirl up into the air. It's dashed away by a sharp wind that rips down the mountain before you. You slap your hands together and smile.

'This is a good place to become a hero.' Your voice is a bit raspy from the dry air.

Your horse neighs. The sound echoes. Quick as a flash, you pull your sword and look around. Behind you, you hear the *clippety-clop* of your horse. You turn around just in time to see it run down the mountain the way you came.

You're all alone. Just you and your sword stand before the legendary Mount Fate . . . and whatever scared your horse.

GO ON TO THE NEXT PAGE.

TWISTED JOURNEYS®

#4

THE TREASURE OF

MOUNT FATE

LERNER BOOKS · MINNEAPOLIS

Story by Jeff Limke

Pencils and inks by Clint Hilinski

Colouring by Hi-Fi Design

Lettering by Marshall Dillon and Terri Delgado

Graphic Universe™ is a trademark and Twisted Journeys® is a registered trademark
of Lerner Publishing Group, Inc.

First published in the United Kingdom in 2008 by
Lerner Books,
Dalton House.
60 Windsor Avenue,
London SW19 2RR

Website address: www.lernerbooks.co.uk

This edition was updated and edited for UK publication by Discovery Books Ltd.,
Unit 3, 37 Watling Street, Leintwardine, Shropshire SY7 0LW

British Library Cataloguing in Publication Data

The treasure of Mount Fate. - (Twisted journeys)
    1. Quests (Expeditions) - Comic books, strips, etc. -
    Juvenile fiction 2. Fantasy comic books, strips, etc.
    3. Children's stories - Comic books, strips, etc.
    741.5

    ISBN-13: 978 1 58013 495 8

Printed in China

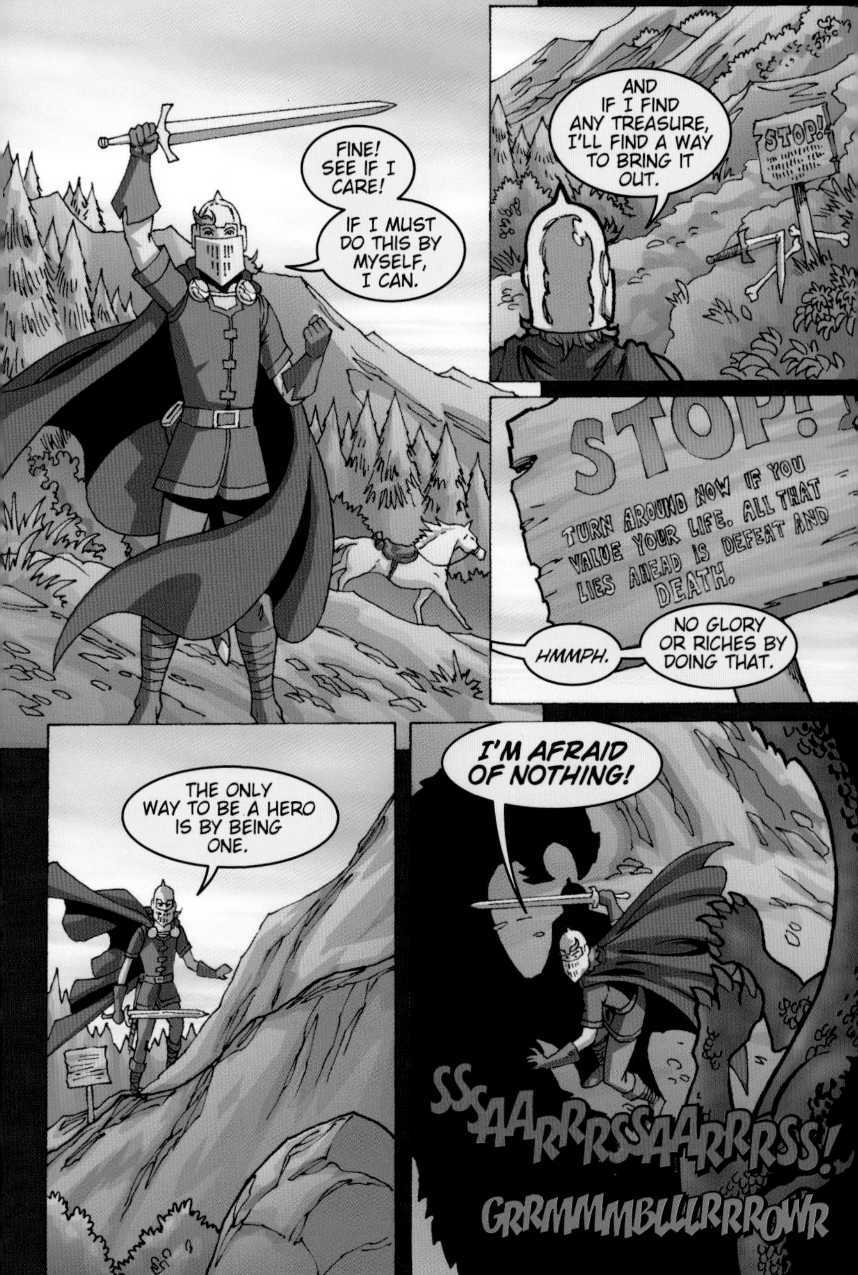
FINE! SEE IF I CARE!
IF I MUST DO THIS BY MYSELF, I CAN.
AND IF I FIND ANY TREASURE, I'LL FIND A WAY TO BRING IT OUT.
STOP!
STOP!
TURN AROUND NOW IF YOU VALUE YOUR LIFE. ALL THAT LIES AHEAD IS DEFEAT AND DEATH.
HMMPH.
NO GLORY OR RICHES BY DOING THAT.
THE ONLY WAY TO BE A HERO IS BY BEING ONE.
I'M AFRAID OF NOTHING!
SSSAARRRSSAARRRSS!
GRRMMMBLLLRRROWR

You're huffing and puffing by the time the trail ends. Where's the entrance to the caves? The old man in the tavern didn't lie to you, did he?

You tap your foot on the rocky ground and stare up at the sky. It's here, it has to be here. *I just have to look a bit,* you tell yourself. *Poke around a little.*

You push aside a few branches. Behind them is a small hole. It's too small to walk into standing up, but if you bend over or crawl, it'll be easy. You smile again. The cold air that stings your cheeks doesn't bother you any-more.

But behind you, you hear noises. You whirl around. It's a borkadrac!

GO ON TO THE NEXT PAGE.

The fearsome and hungry borkadrac moves towards you, hissing. In the village below the mountain, you heard that no one escapes this beast.

WILL YOU...

...pull your sword to fight off this monster?

TURN TO PAGE 42.

...turn and run towards the cave opening?

TURN TO PAGE 54.

Great, more spiders. The only choice
is which ones to fight.

WILL YOU...

face the little spiders?
TURN TO PAGE 93.

face the big spider?
TURN TO PAGE 109.

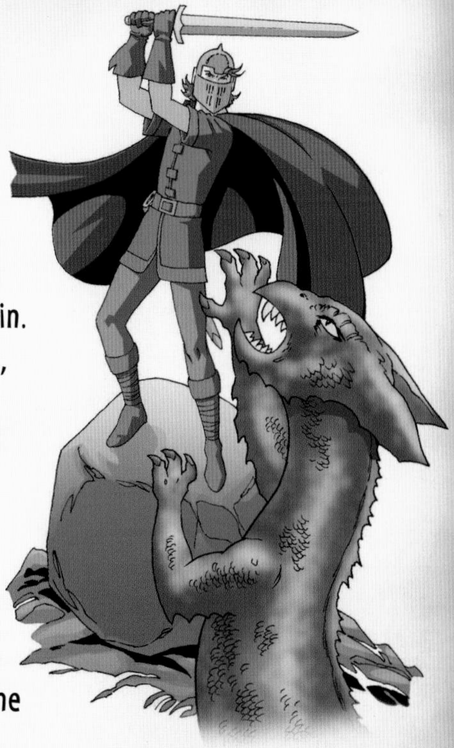

You climb up the rock. It will be harder for the borkadrac to hit you up here.

The borkadrac steps from the bushes, mouth partially open in a sinister grin. Your eyes lock on it. It hisses, spitting the sound as though air is leaking from inside it.

'You want me?' you shout. 'Come and get me!'

It growls and charges forwards, leaping upwards at the last second.

You swing your sword down, missing. The borkadrac's claw strikes your bad ankle. The pain rips through you and you stumble.

The sword falls from your hand as you reach out and try to grab the rock to get your balance. You feel yourself slipping backwards. Your hands scramble for a handhold, but they don't find one.

The last thing you see is the borkadrac. It looks over the edge of the cliff down at you as you fall away from it, the mountain and the mountain's treasure.

THE END

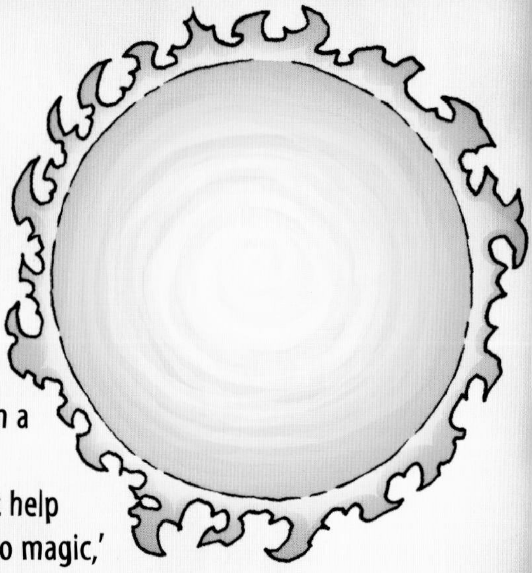

The heat of the fireball scratches at your neck, stinging as it increases. Maybe you're just tired, but you swear you can hear Alaric's voice from a lesson long ago.

'Fighting skills won't help much when it comes to magic,' he says. 'Sometimes escape is just a matter of luck.'

Now you hear his deep-throated chuckle. 'Of course, anyone who's bothered to put a magic trap in your path probably also made sure you wouldn't get very lucky....'

The polished walls of the hallway magnify the light and heat. You squint as you try to see where you're running. You bang against a wall. It's cool to the touch, and it is incredibly tempting to press yourself against it.

The roaring sound of the fireball behind you brings you back to your senses.

GO ON TO THE NEXT PAGE.

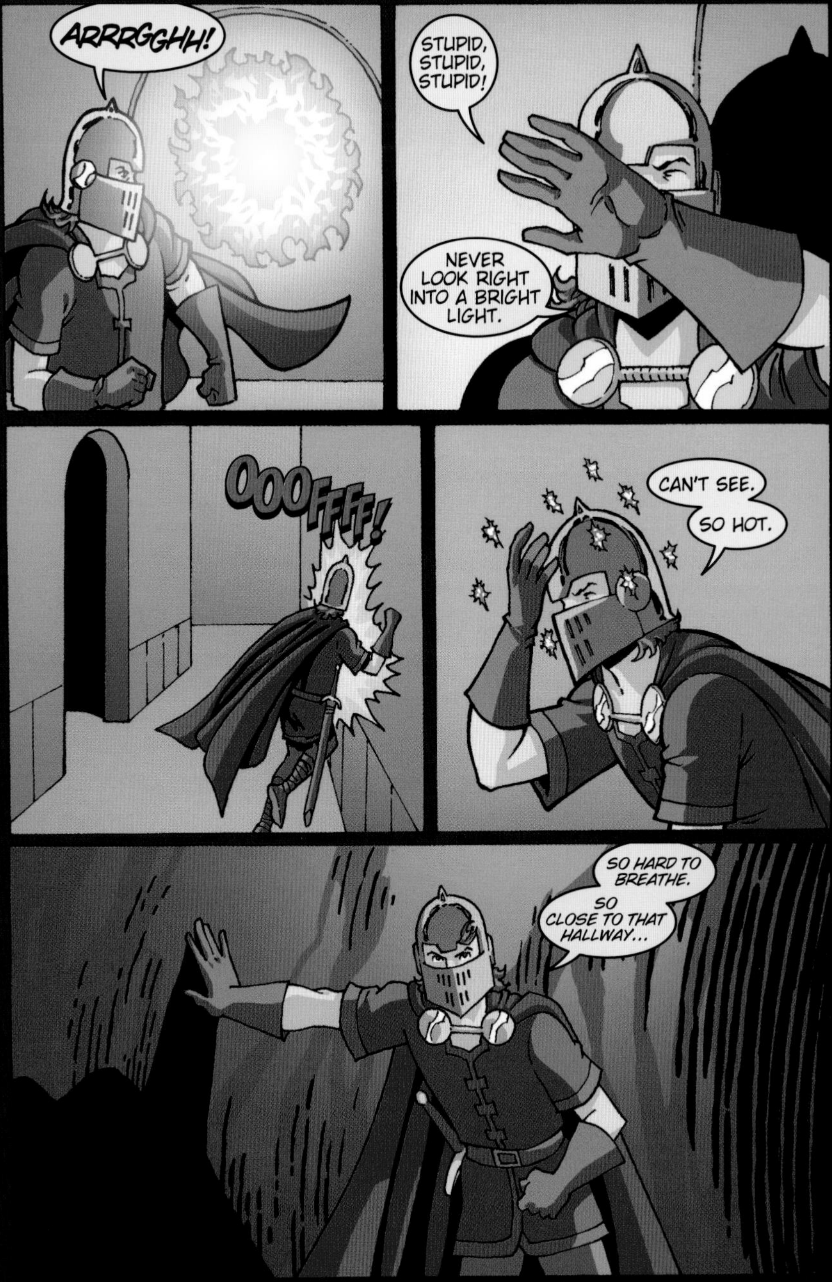
ARRRGGHH!
STUPID, STUPID, STUPID!
NEVER LOOK RIGHT INTO A BRIGHT LIGHT.
OOOFFFF!
CAN'T SEE.
SO HOT.
SO HARD TO BREATHE.
SO CLOSE TO THAT HALLWAY...

GO ON TO THE NEXT PAGE.

Maybe you should lie down. Heat rises, so the floor may be the safest place to be. But the entrance to the other hallway is only a bit further. It's maybe two steps and a leap.

WILL YOU...

...make a run for the entrance?

TURN TO PAGE 52.

...press yourself flat against the floor?

TURN TO PAGE 70.

'RRRAAAWWWRRR!' you scream as you run in, hoping to scare the dragon.

Behind you, you hear Wizard Uchawi say, 'That's not a good idea.'

'Silly, silly adventurer. You wish to be a hero, so you attack a dragon by yourself.' The words echo off the walls.

You feel the air around you whip about, and you see the dragon spread his wings. They're twice as wide as he is big. You swing at one, but you're too slow and too far away.

You turn to look back at the wizard, but all you can see is a golden, glowing globe of light where he should be. 'Wizard?' you yell.

'Too late now,' you hear him call back.

'I would agree with the wizard. You should have talked first, then acted.' Gartrugh's voice seems to come from all around.

The air goes warm, and you know what's going to happen next.

GO ON TO THE NEXT PAGE.

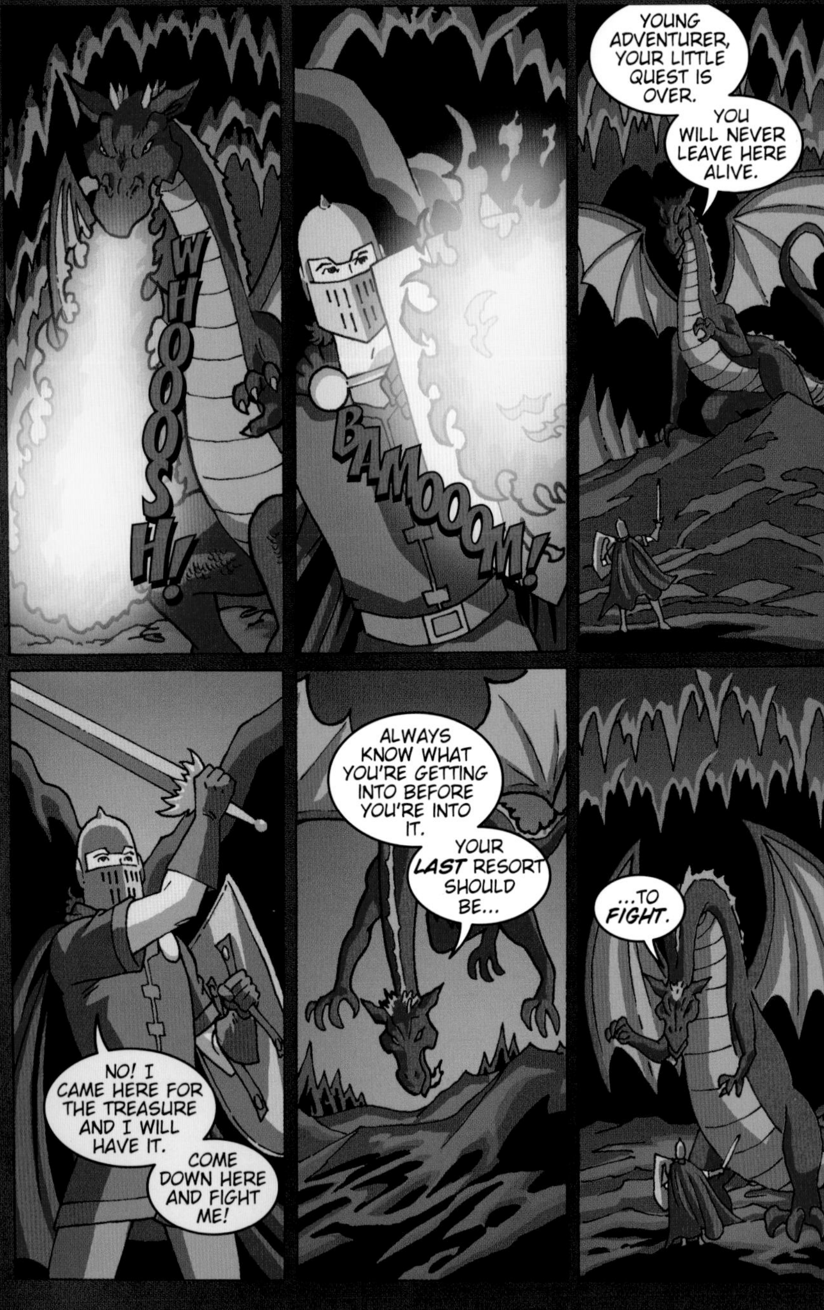
WHOOOOSH!
BAMOOOOM!
YOUNG ADVENTURER, YOUR LITTLE QUEST IS OVER.
YOU WILL NEVER LEAVE HERE ALIVE.
NO! I CAME HERE FOR THE TREASURE AND I WILL HAVE IT.
COME DOWN HERE AND FIGHT ME!
ALWAYS KNOW WHAT YOU'RE GETTING INTO BEFORE YOU'RE INTO IT.
YOUR LAST RESORT SHOULD BE...
...TO FIGHT.

GO ON TO THE NEXT PAGE.

You realise
Gartrugh is right. He's
much too big for you to have
ever defeated with your sword,
even though it's magic.

But you've issued your challenge, and
not to back it up would not be heroic.

You step forwards as you slash your sword before you.
The dragon dances backwards, but not in fear.

'I gave you a chance not to fight me, but still you
choose to,' Gartrugh says with a sigh. 'I do not like this,
but you force me to defend myself.'

Now, you charge forwards, swinging your sword to and
fro and hear the dragon breathe inward. *Here it comes,*
you tell yourself.

And you're right. The flame comes down and the
last thing you feel is the singeing heat of Gartrugh's
flaming breath.

THE END

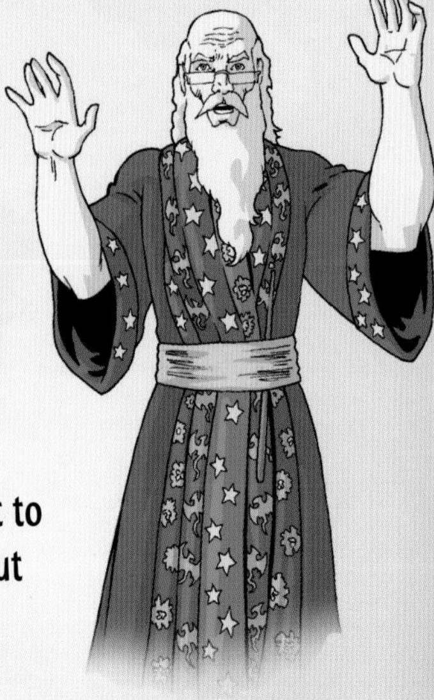

'What do you mean, you don't know? What's to know?' Wizard Uchawi's neck starts turning red. The colour seems to be moving up towards his face. 'Do you know how long I've been stuck here?'

You shake your head. You're afraid to help him and afraid not to help him. What if he's lying about being trapped?

'Hello? Is anyone in there?' Wizard Uchawi taps you on the head with his staff. 'Do you need some help making a decision?'

'I'm not sure,' you say. You hear the bear roar and the birds screech.

'No one ever knows for sure, but time is running out, and in fact it may be too late.'

'What do you mean?'

'I mean, those doors will disappear and you'll be stuck here, too. The spell that keeps me here affects all who enter this room.'

You feel your neck turn red, then your face. 'WHAT!'

GO ON TO THE NEXT PAGE.

You're about to be trapped! But there's a door just a few strides away.

'Go ahead. You're probably quicker than I am.' A tear flows down Wizard Uchawi's cheek. 'I'll just sit down and play solitaire a few more times...'

WILL YOU...

...rush to the door before your time runs out?

TURN TO PAGE 94.

...stop to grab Wizard Uchawi?

TURN TO PAGE 103.

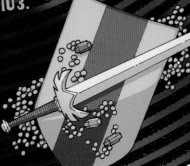

You swing your sword. The borkadrac twists away in defence, but instead of pushing forwards with the sword, you turn and run. Behind you, the beast howls, realizing it has been tricked.

The ground thumps and you hear the bushes cracking and breaking behind you as the beast chases you. *Just keep running, pump the arms,* you tell yourself. *Get some distance between you and this...this thing.*

Its hisses sound closer. A branch flies by your right ear, scratching your cheek. You check over your shoulder. The borkadrac is just three paces behind, but it's not getting any closer. It's big, but at least it's not very fast.

Ahead, the road turns left and the bushes gets thicker. There are trees to climb. You should be able to lose the beast there if you can just get out of sight. Everyone knows borkadracs see better than they smell.

GO ON TO THE NEXT PAGE.

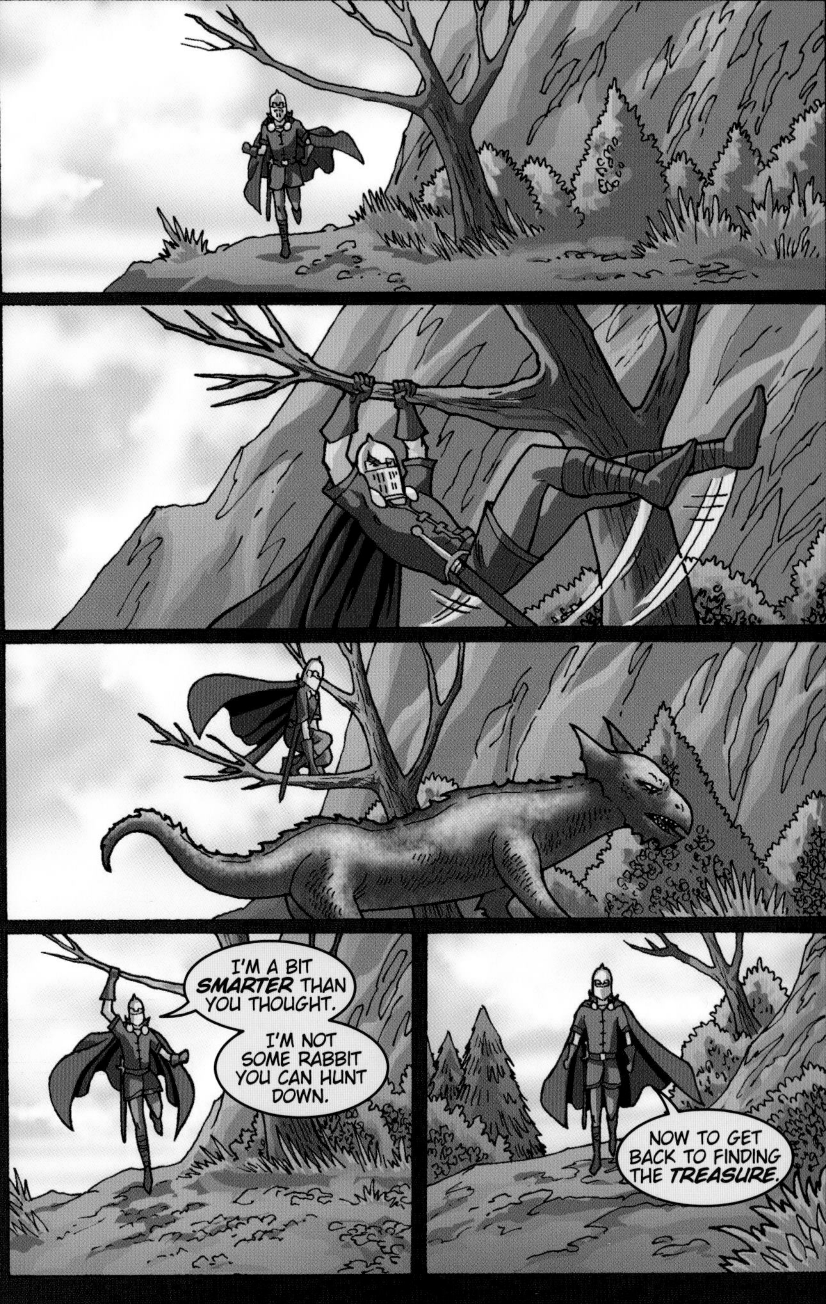
I'M A BIT SMARTER THAN YOU THOUGHT.
I'M NOT SOME RABBIT YOU CAN HUNT DOWN.
NOW TO GET BACK TO FINDING THE TREASURE.

GO ON TO THE NEXT PAGE.

The trail branches here. The left branch is wider, while the right branch is overgrown with plants.

Wait, what's that snapping noise behind you? Oh no, it's the borkadrac!

WILL YOU...

... turn to face the borkadrac once and for all?
TURN TO PAGE 30.

...take the path to the right?
TURN TO PAGE 39.

...take the path to the left?
TURN TO PAGE 74.

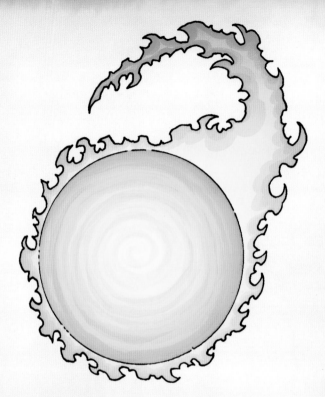

It missed you before and it might miss you again.

Then again, it must have *known* it missed you or it wouldn't be coming back, wouldn't it?

You press yourself against the wall and try to make yourself as small as possible.

There's no time to run away now. The roaring is loud. It's making your ears ring again.

That ringing is the last thing you hear, as the fireball is very thorough, leaving nothing behind it – not even ash.

THE END

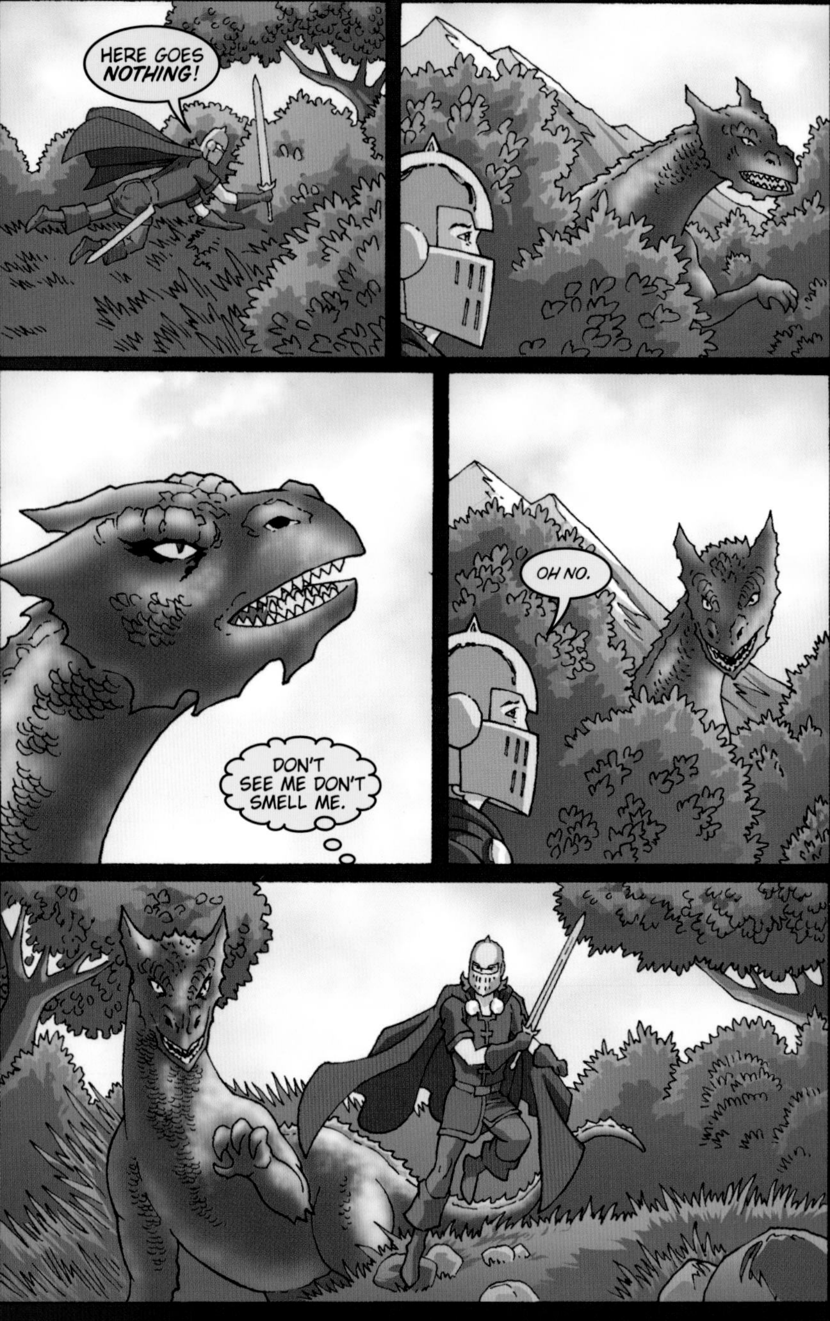
HERE GOES NOTHING!
DON'T SEE ME DON'T SMELL ME.
OH NO.

GO ON TO THE NEXT PAGE.

Keep running, you tell yourself, *just keep running.* The beast is too big to catch up on this path, you hope. You can hear it lumbering about through the bushes. It won't surprise you, that's for sure.

Ahead you spy daylight through the bushes. That's good. You must be close to the goats' grazing pasture. That means people – and the borkadrac isn't stupid enough to venture out where people could hunt it.

Just a few more metres. Your lungs feel like they're on fire. Your feet are sore. You step forwards and feel your foot catch on a root.

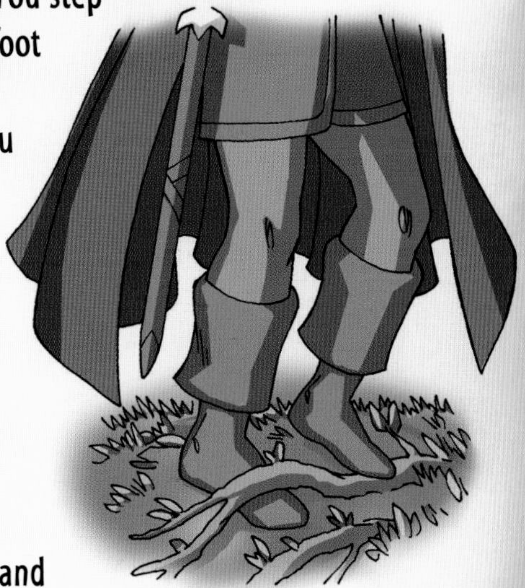

Down you tumble. You flail your hands out to catch yourself.

WHOOMP!

You land in a heap. Your ankle feels like someone hit it with a club. But you've got to get up. GOT TO GET UP!

You push yourself up and half run, half stumble towards the blue sky ahead.

You rush towards the sky — only to realise that the path ends here. You're at the edge of a cliff. Nothing but a big rock stands between you and a very long fall.

WILL YOU...

...climb the rock to fight the borkadrac?
TURN TO PAGE 9.

...stand your ground?
TURN TO PAGE 41.

You turn and run. Your heart beats like a hammer and your breathing is harsh. The air is hot and smells of sulphur. You pump your arms hard. Your feet pound the ground. This is a race for your life.

And you have to hope Wizard Uchawi won't be cross. Why would he be? You only abandoned him, condemned him to stay in that room alone until someone else comes along. Of course, no one else ever will come along because you're going to find the treasure. And once the treasure is gone, no one will have any reason to come here, ever again.

Well, that's how it would have gone if you hadn't spun that stupid wheel, you snarl at yourself.

Sweat drips down your forehead and into your eyes, where it stings. For a second you can't see anything, but you keep running, hoping you don't run into –

WHAM!

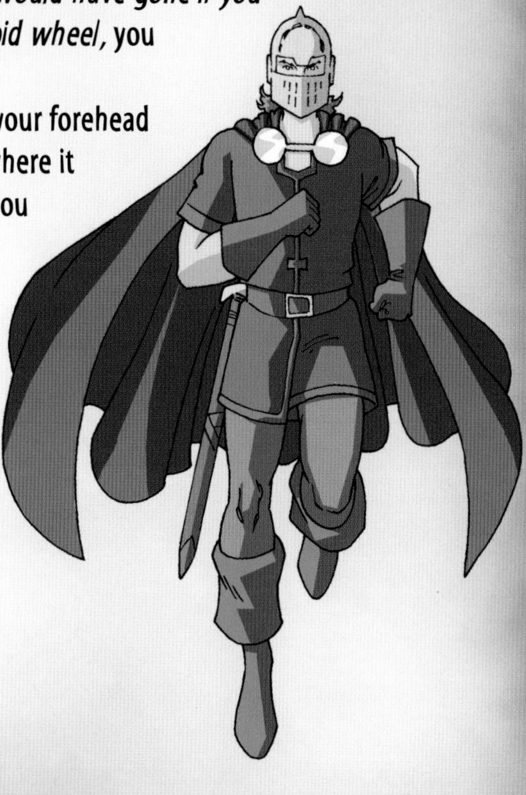

GO ON TO THE NEXT PAGE.

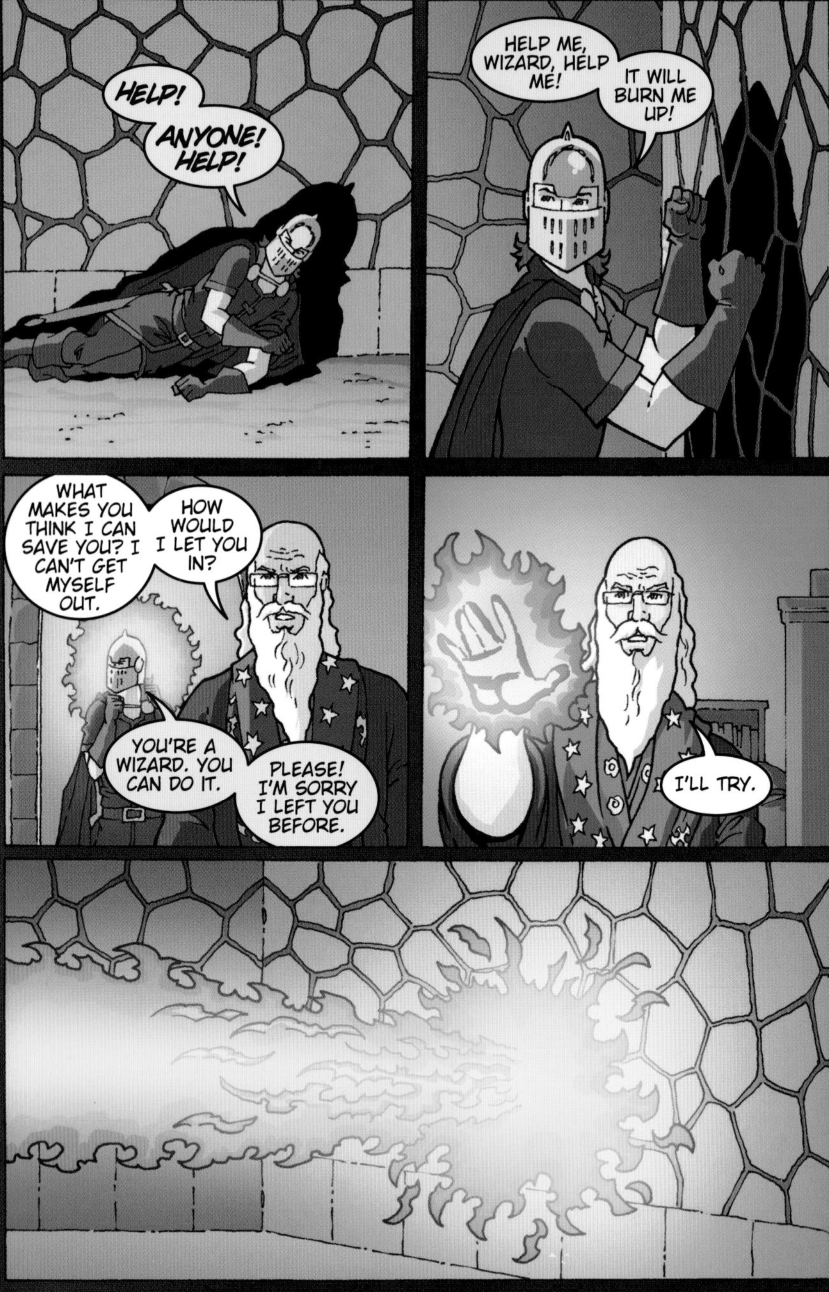
HELP!
ANYONE! HELP!
HELP ME, WIZARD, HELP ME!
IT WILL BURN ME UP!
WHAT MAKES YOU THINK I CAN SAVE YOU? I CAN'T GET MYSELF OUT.
HOW WOULD I LET YOU IN?
YOU'RE A WIZARD. YOU CAN DO IT.
PLEASE! I'M SORRY I LEFT YOU BEFORE.
I'LL TRY.

GO ON TO THE NEXT PAGE.

'I hope you're not looking for conversation. I'm not very happy with you.' Wizard Uchawi knocks you on the head with his staff. It hurts and you realise you hadn't seen the staff before. You look around and realise the room seems bigger now, filled with more objects...

...except for a small section on the far side, where a table and a chair sit forlornly.

'Over there. That's your space.'

'I said I was sorry. I was wrong.' You can't look at him. You're too ashamed.

'That's a good start. We have some time to get over this "misunderstanding".'

'How long do we have?'

'I waited nine hundred years for you.' Wizard Uchawi plops onto his chair and purses his lips.

Your jaw drops. 'Nine hundred years? I'll be dead.'

Wizard Uchawi smirks, then goes back to frowning. 'Oh no, we don't age in here. We have all the time we'll need.'

THE END

You hated to say no, but it was the only way to get out of the room in time before the doors disappeared.

The echo of Wizard Uchawi yelling 'Nooooooooo' still rings in your ears. He seemed like a likeable fellow, but he was too old and too slow.

The air here is dryer, a bit warm, too. Ahead you see a sharp turn, like the one where you found your magic sword. You wonder what's beyond this one. Maybe magic armour?

Instead, you see another turn in the passage, but it's not empty. There's a flat wheel stuck in the ground and a shield emblem beside it. Bricks along the wheel's edges follow a pattern: sword, blank brick, sword, blank brick.

The wheel spins when you touch it, then stops. The shield points at a blank brick.

The air suddenly gets warmer and you hear a roaring sound.

GO ON TO THE NEXT PAGE.

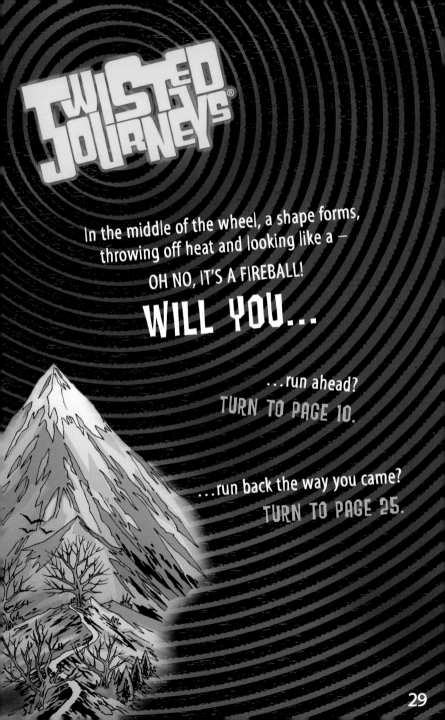

In the middle of the wheel, a shape forms, throwing off heat and looking like a —

OH NO, IT'S A FIREBALL!

WILL YOU...

...run ahead?
TURN TO PAGE 10.

...run back the way you came?
TURN TO PAGE 25.

You step forwards, keeping your weight on the balls of your feet so you can react quickly. You hold the sword in front of you in a two-handed grip to allow you to block an attack from any side.

You hold your breath, listening for any sound. Nothing. Nothing's moving. You exhale and –

An explosion of twigs, leaves, dirt and growls bursts through the bushes on your left. You turn and ready your sword, but you're too late. The borkadrac's foul-smelling mouth is the last thing you see or smell.

THE END

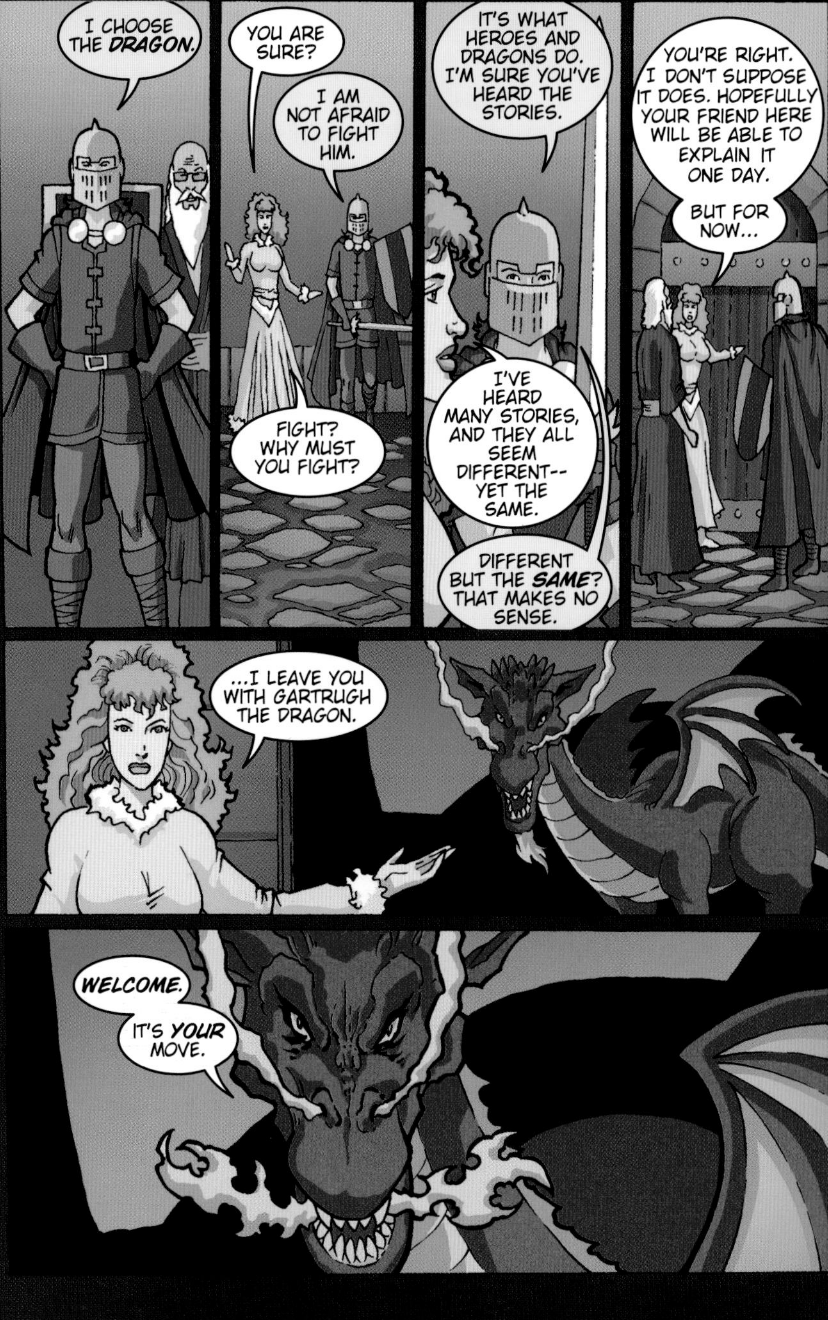
I CHOOSE THE *DRAGON.*
YOU ARE SURE?
I AM NOT AFRAID TO FIGHT HIM.
FIGHT? WHY MUST YOU FIGHT?
IT'S WHAT HEROES AND DRAGONS DO. I'M SURE YOU'VE HEARD THE STORIES.
I'VE HEARD MANY STORIES, AND THEY ALL SEEM DIFFERENT-- YET THE SAME.
DIFFERENT BUT THE *SAME*? THAT MAKES NO SENSE.
YOU'RE RIGHT. I DON'T SUPPOSE IT DOES. HOPEFULLY YOUR FRIEND HERE WILL BE ABLE TO EXPLAIN IT ONE DAY.
BUT FOR NOW...
...I LEAVE YOU WITH GARTRUGH THE DRAGON.
WELCOME.
IT'S *YOUR* MOVE.

GO ON TO THE NEXT PAGE.

TWISTED JOURNEYS®

Gartrugh's voice sounds like a hissing snake crossed with a bass drum. But what scares you more than the flames is that he spoke to you. Nobody told you dragons could do that.

WILL YOU...

...pull your sword to fight?

TURN TO PAGE 13.

...run away to save yourself?

TURN TO PAGE 36.

...walk in without drawing your sword?

TURN TO PAGE 89.

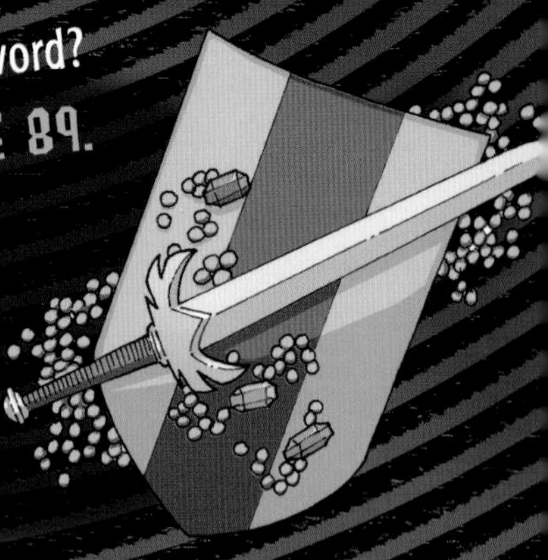

You grip your shield and sword so tightly, your knuckles turn white. You swing, the air singing with the sound of metal cleaving stone and the thud of weapons hitting your shield. Three, five, eight soldiers fall before you, but more keep coming.

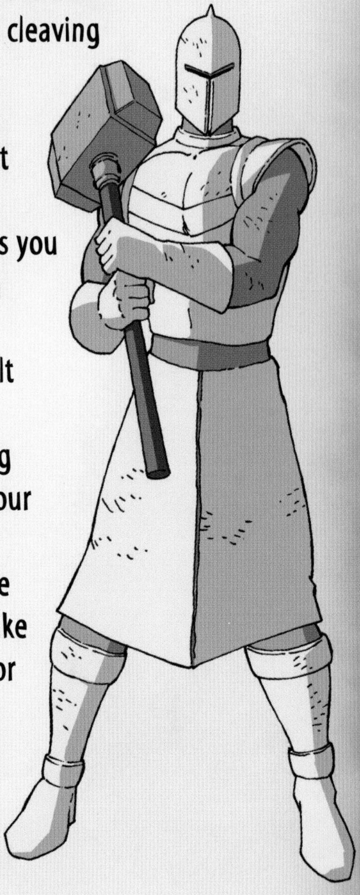

A sharp pain in your leg makes you wince. You look down and see a small cut. That isn't what hurts though...Your leg is changing. It looks like stone.

You keep fighting, but your leg doesn't move easily. Nor does your foot.

Oh no. You realise where these soldiers came from. They were like you once, adventurers looking for treasure. They fought the stone army in this hallway, just as you are fighting now.

You stop fighting and stand still. The soldiers stop, too. Every one of them understands: You are the newest stone soldier to join this little army forever.

THE END

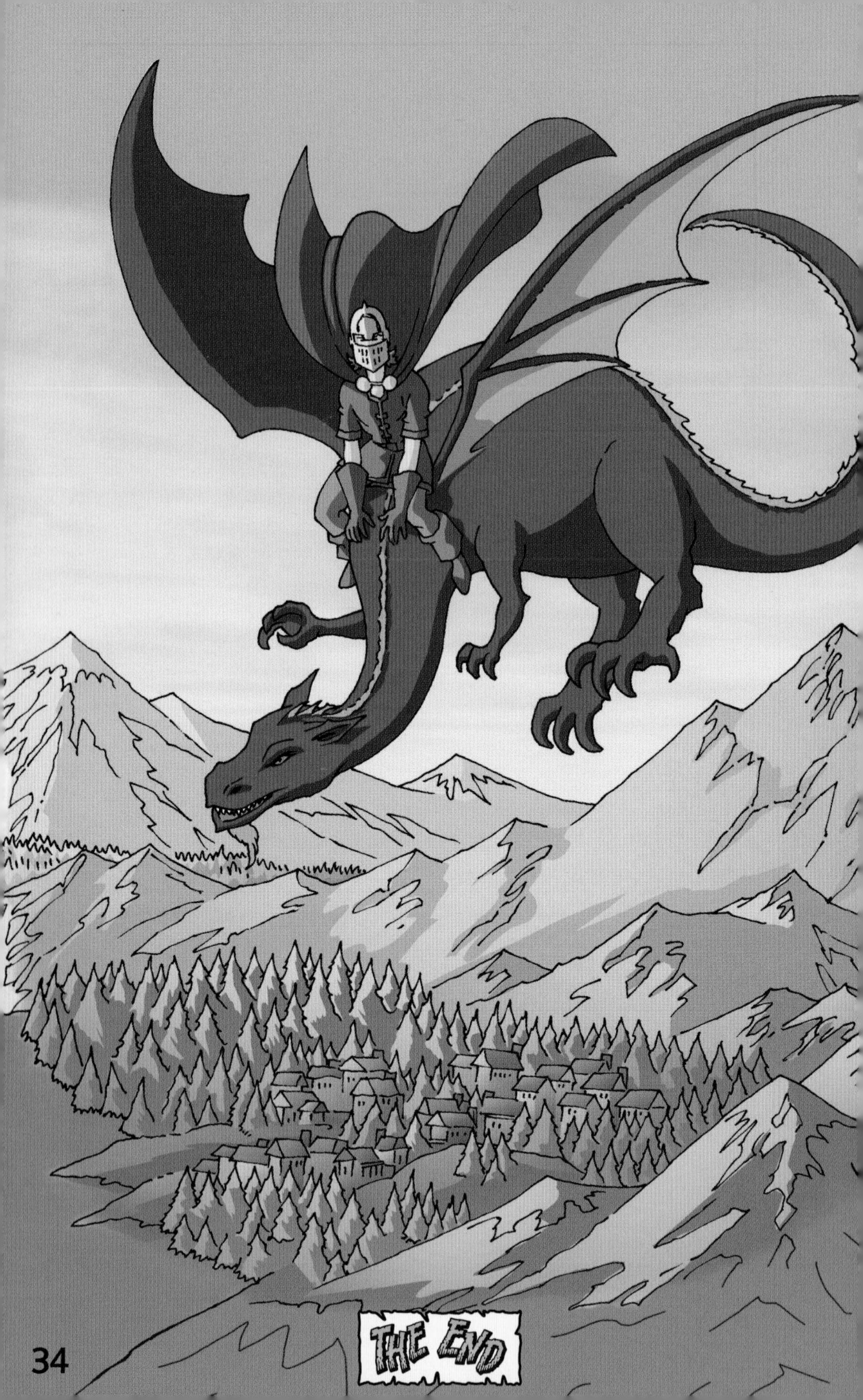
THE END

You rub the lamp three times. It grows warm, then shakes and twists, trying to break free.

'Tell the genie to come out,' yells Wizard Uchawi.

'I command you, genie, as your master, to come out!' The room fills with thunder and a whirling wind.

The genie bows. 'What would you have me do, master, for your first of three wishes?'

'I wish to have all the treasure packed for travel and for you to send those heroes home safely,' you say.

'Very good.' The genie claps. The treasure appears, packed in carts pulled by mules and the heroes vanish. 'And what of your next wish?'

You wink at the wizard. 'All in good time, genie.'

'I agree. You have chosen well, young hero,' says the Lady of the Mount, who has appeared suddenly from out of thin air.

You point towards the door. 'Time for us to go home rich and famous, Uchawi,' you say as the mules begin walking.

THE END

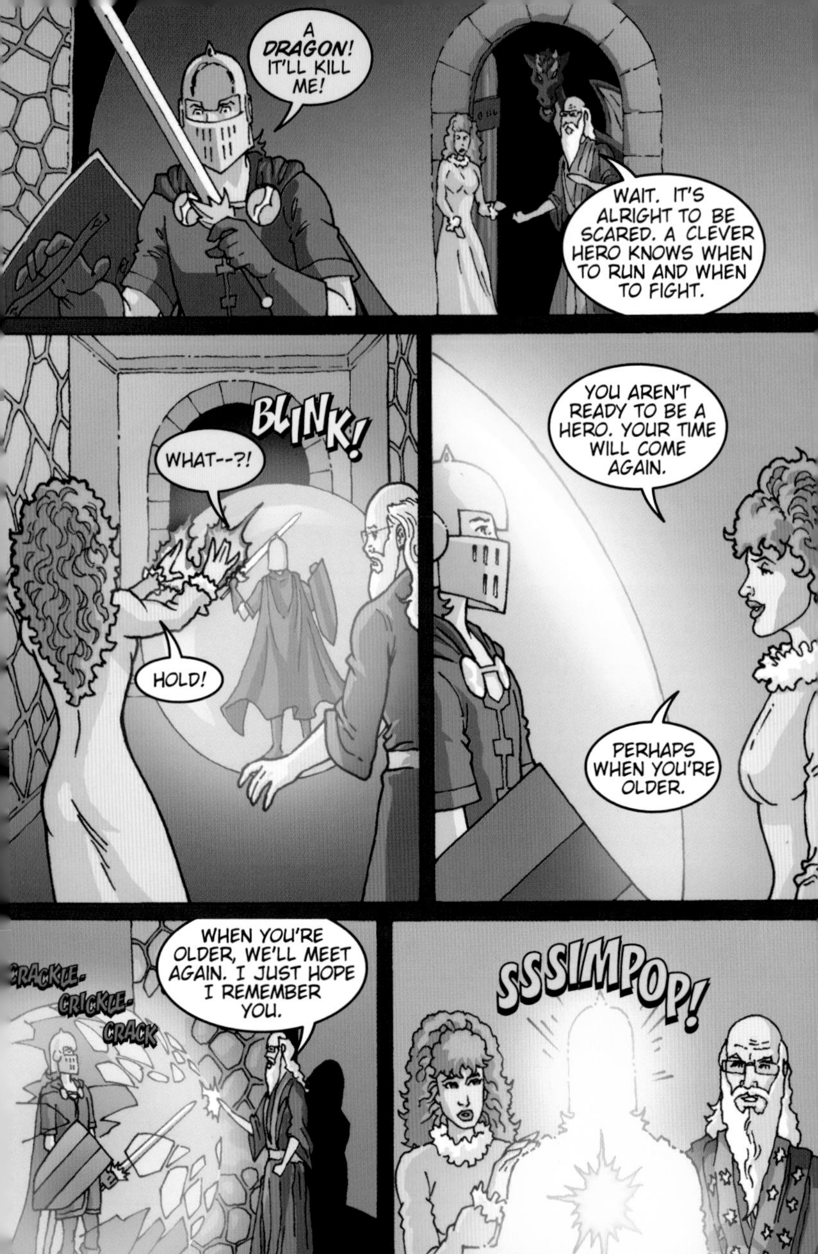
A DRAGON! IT'LL KILL ME!
WAIT. IT'S ALRIGHT TO BE SCARED. A CLEVER HERO KNOWS WHEN TO RUN AND WHEN TO FIGHT.
BLINK!
WHAT--?!
HOLD!
YOU AREN'T READY TO BE A HERO. YOUR TIME WILL COME AGAIN.
PERHAPS WHEN YOU'RE OLDER.
CRACKLE-
CRICKLE-
CRACK
WHEN YOU'RE OLDER, WE'LL MEET AGAIN. I JUST HOPE I REMEMBER YOU.
SSSIMPOP!

The cockerel's crowing wakes you. As you rub your eyes, you think, *What a strange dream.*

Once dressed, you make your way to breakfast. Your mother stands over a pot, stirring. 'I had a very odd dream,' you tell her.

She smiles. 'Tell me about it.'

You sit down on the wooden bench as she ladles porridge into a bowl in front of you. 'Well, I was older and wanting to be a hero, so I went to find the treasure of Mount Fate.'

Your mother crinkles her eyebrows. 'Mount Fate? That's a dangerous place.'

'It was only a dream, Mother.' You drone on about the wizard and the Lady of the Mount. But in your mind you're thinking: Someday when you're older and Alaric has taught you more, you're going to go there and find that treasure.

Yes, that would be quite the adventure.

THE END

No wonder the sword is so light. It's magic. Good thing — the stone soldiers are closing in. Over your shoulder, you spot a door behind you that you hadn't noticed.

WILL YOU...

...quickly check the door?
TURN TO PAGE 75.

...keep shuffling backwards and ignore the door?
TURN TO PAGE 96.

The borkadrac doesn't follow you. Everything seems peaceful. The mountain birds chirp a little song, and bees are buzzing.

SNAP! Something snags your ankle. You're knocked backwards and your left leg is yanked upwards. You smack your head on the ground. Things go a bit blurry.

Seconds later, you're staring down at the ground where you had stood. You realise you're hanging from a tree branch, bobbing by your leg. Someone must have laid a trap on this path. Well, you'll just take your sword and cut –

Wait, your sword isn't in your hand. Where is it?

You tilt your head back, and there it is. On the path below. Out of reach.

Just as you begin to shout for help, you see some bones to the side of the road. Looks like you weren't the first one to make the wrong choice on this trail.

THE END

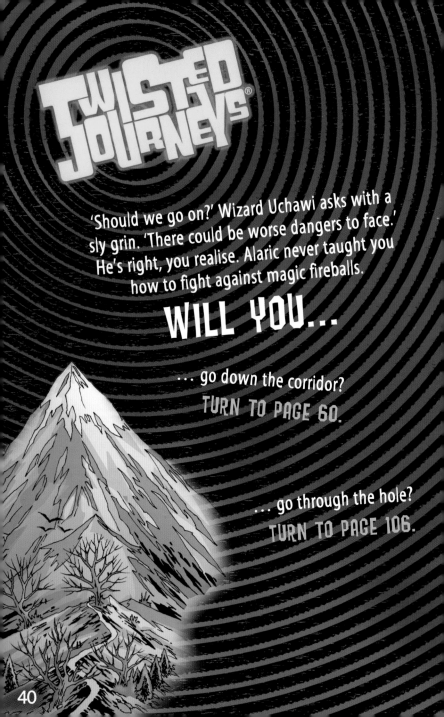

'Should we go on?' Wizard Uchawi asks with a sly grin. 'There could be worse dangers to face.' He's right, you realise. Alaric never taught you how to fight against magic fireballs.

WILL YOU...

... go down the corridor?
TURN TO PAGE 60.

... go through the hole?
TURN TO PAGE 106.

You plant your feet wide, grip the sword in two hands and raise it over your head. Your ankle throbs in pain.

Emerging from the bushes, the borkadrac sees you and charges. It swipes at you, claws extended. You swing the sword down. The edge of the blade cuts into the monster's paw.

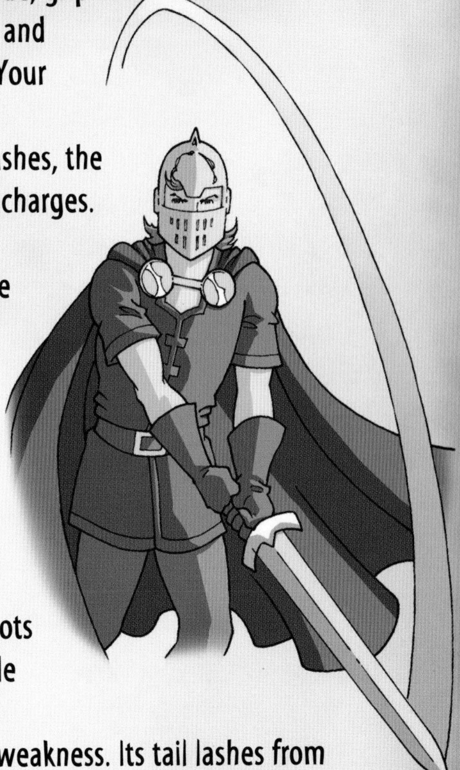

The borkadrac roars in pain as you pull back the sword, pivoting on your feet. Your ankle protests. Pain shoots up your leg. You stumble but catch yourself.

The beast spots your weakness. Its tail lashes from the side. It strikes your calf, pulling your leg out from under you and sending you to the ground. Your sword slips from your grip and clatters just out of reach.

The borkadrac moves forward with slow steps, mouth wide, saliva dripping. Its tongue snakes about.

Now, unfortunately, you'll learn the answer to the question of whether it will eat you in one bite or two.

THE END

You draw your sword and swing, just like your mentor, Alaric the Brave, taught you. Of course, you fought only little kobolds when he trained you, not hungry borkadracs. But this is how Alaric earned his name, and now you will too.

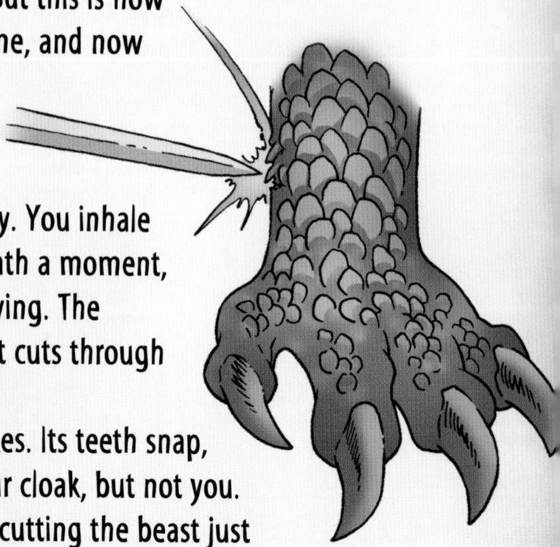

The borkadrac's breath smells rotten, and his skin looks oily. You inhale deeply, hold the breath a moment, and exhale as you swing. The sword whooshes as it cuts through the air. You miss!

The borkadrac strikes. Its teeth snap, snagging a bit of your cloak, but not you. You turn and swing, cutting the beast just above one leg. Your sword catches in the borkadrac's scales and throws you off balance. You stumble and catch yourself, but the beast is already moving towards you.

GO ON TO THE NEXT PAGE.

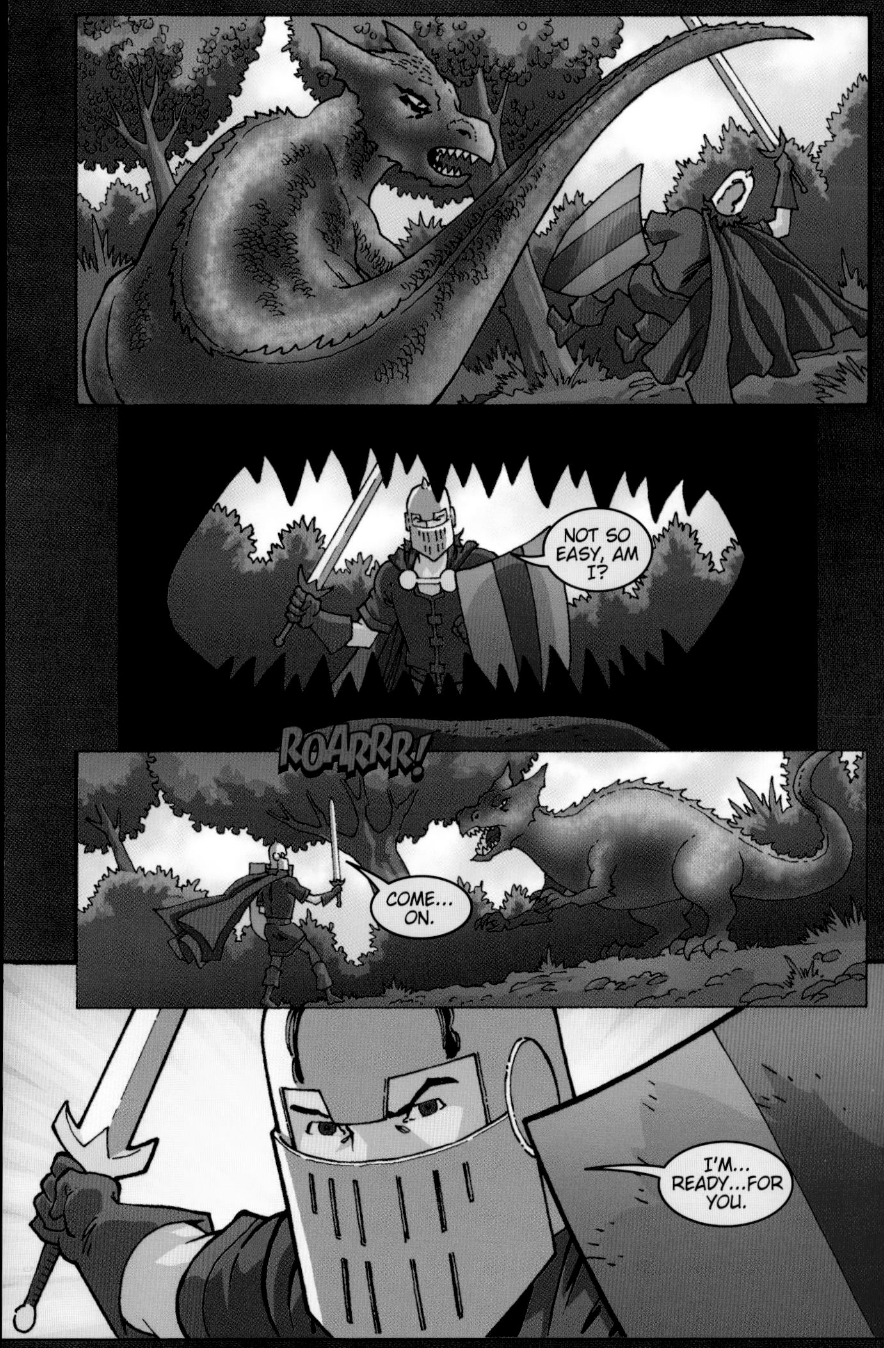
NOT SO EASY, AM I?
ROARRR!
COME... ON.
I'M... READY...FOR YOU.

GO ON TO THE NEXT PAGE.

TWISTED JOURNEYS®

You're using every piece of the training you received from Alaric. But you don't know how long it — or you — will last.

WILL YOU...

...turn and run down the path away from the borkadrac?

TURN TO PAGE 71.

...continue this fight?

TURN TO PAGE 18.

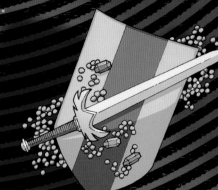

The Lady of the Mount touches your head. Everything goes white.

You open your eyes. It's dark, but you can still see. Catching a whiff of the air, you cough.

'My thoughts, too,' says Wizard Uchawi, who is standing next to you.

Around you, everything twinkles. Diamonds seem to be scattered about. In fact, it looks as though some are hanging in the air, like stars. That doesn't seem right.

Something wet spatters your arm, dripping slowly. It burns a little. You try to shake it off. It sticks, not much coming loose at all. The bit that does hits the ground with a disgusting 'plop'.

Wizard Uchawi lights up his wand. What you see is unbelievable. Huge blobs of clear, murky ooze glop about. Inside the ooze you can see coins, gems, rocks, dirt and — no, that can't be right. But it is. Those are bones. Human bones.

GO ON TO THE NEXT PAGE.

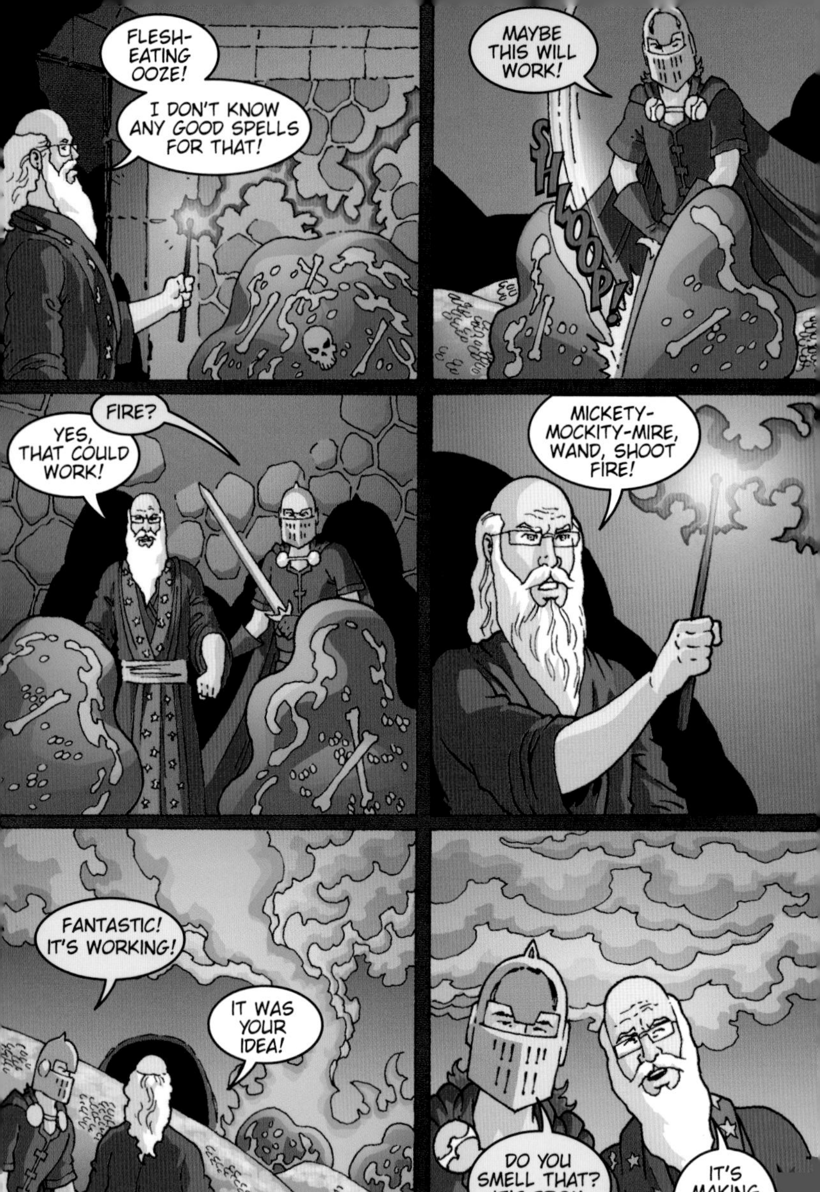
FLESH-EATING OOZE!
I DON'T KNOW ANY GOOD SPELLS FOR THAT!
MAYBE THIS WILL WORK!
SHLOOP!
FIRE?
YES, THAT COULD WORK!
MICKETY-MOCKITY-MIRE, WAND, SHOOT FIRE!
FANTASTIC! IT'S WORKING!
IT WAS YOUR IDEA!
DO YOU SMELL THAT? IT'S FROM THEM.
IT'S MAKING ME FEEL FUNNY.

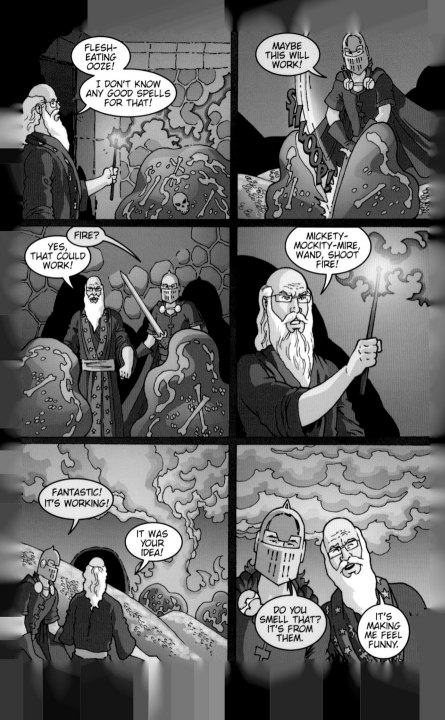

The smoky air burns as you breathe it. It's hard to keep your eyes open. When you try, the air burns them, making them water. Your joints feel weak, like you have the flu.

You cough hard. Your lungs burn and your throat is raw. The fire was a bad idea. The smoke has poisoned the air.

As you blink, tears run down the side of your face. You look at Wizard Uchawi, but he's not moving. You push his shoulder. He still doesn't move. He seems asleep.

You try to stand, but your legs don't work and you feel tired. Just a little nap to get your strength. That's all you need.

You close your eyes, never to wake up again.

THE END

You press the up arrow and the doors open to reveal a spiral staircase leading up. The steps are moving, so all you have to do is hop on.

'Pretty nifty,' says Wizard Uchawi. 'I'd heard about these but never expected to see one. Doesn't use magic, you know?'

You're not interested. The stairs move up, and soon you can see the sky above you. You feel a bit dizzy from the turning. At the top, you step off onto a small platform.

The air is cold, and you can see your breath. You're standing on the top of Mount Fate. Wizard Uchawi stands beside you. 'Thanks,' he says as he begins to glow and float upward. 'Make sure to look me up if you're ever in River City,' he yells back at you. Some of his belongings begins to float after him — a rope, boxes and a birdcage.

It looks as if you'll be stuck up here all alone.

GO ON TO THE NEXT PAGE.

You run alongside, shouting at Wizard Uchawi to stop, but he keeps moving. His belongings, including the rope, are quite close to you, floating like he is.

WILL YOU...

...stop and watch everything fly away?
TURN TO PAGE 95.

...reach out and grab at his rope?
TURN TO PAGE 77.

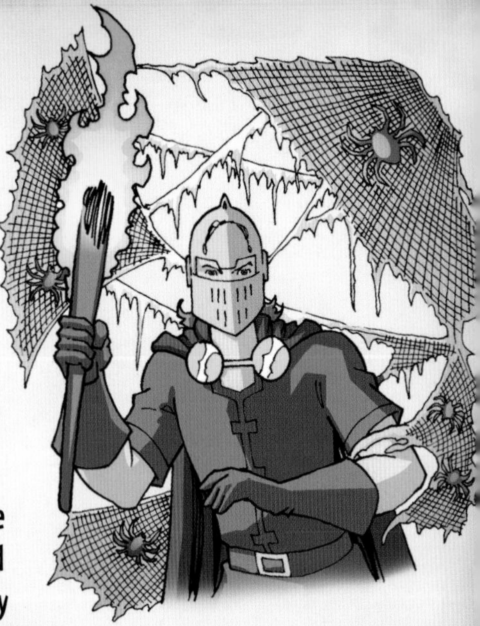

It's wet in here and with every step you feel like you could slip. Sharp stones stick up from the uneven floor. If you fall, they could cut you quite badly.

Every so often, you see a small indentation where sections have been carved out of the rock. Somebody has been mining here. Maybe there really is treasure in this place. Goblins have been known to mine for valuable rocks. This tunnel could very well be a goblin mine.

Just as you're ready to take a step, a flash catches your eye...again. Maybe you'll be lucky twice.

You stop, kneel down and look closely at a shiny spot. It looks like flecks of gold. With the point of your sword, you tap it, dislodging the loose rock around it. YES! IT'S GOLD!

GO ON TO THE NEXT PAGE.

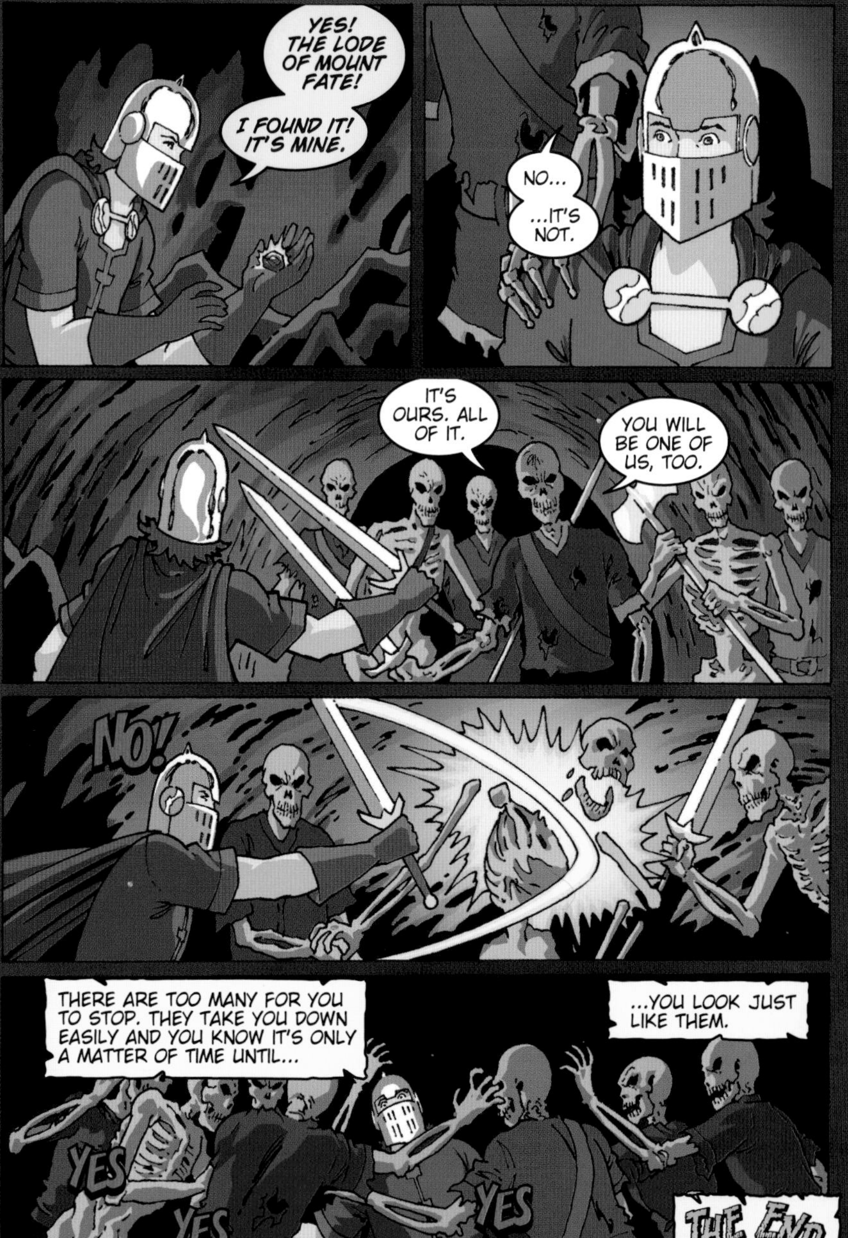

YES! THE LODE OF MOUNT FATE!
I FOUND IT! IT'S MINE.
NO...
...IT'S NOT.
IT'S OURS. ALL OF IT.
YOU WILL BE ONE OF US, TOO.
NO!
THERE ARE TOO MANY FOR YOU TO STOP. THEY TAKE YOU DOWN EASILY AND YOU KNOW IT'S ONLY A MATTER OF TIME UNTIL...
...YOU LOOK JUST LIKE THEM.
YES
YES
YES
THE END

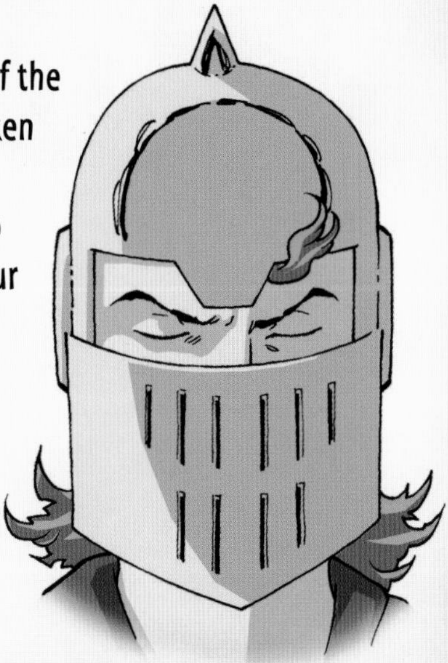

You take what feel like two of the longest steps you have ever taken and dive into the hall.

You cover your ears, trying to block out the fireball's roar. Your ears ring. You press your eyes closed. You inhale deeply and hold it.

A flash of heat bathes you and then passes. Still holding your breath, you wait.

Nothing. No noise. You open one eye. Nothing moves. A torch flickers back to life. You exhale and begin to breathe again. The light of the hallway washes over you. The roar of the fireball seems to be growing fainter, but it's hard to tell with the ringing in your ears. You're sure that if someone were next to you screaming, you wouldn't hear a thing.

But you made it. You survived.

No, wait – the roaring is getting louder…again.

GO ON TO THE NEXT PAGE.

TWISTED JOURNEYS®

It seems impossible – but the fireball is whooshing towards you again! It almost seems to be tracking you.

WILL YOU...

...crawl back deeper into the hallway?

TURN TO PAGE 104.

...stay where you are?

TURN TO PAGE 21.

It's a tight fit, and as you dive into the cave, your cloak snags on a rock. You pull on it. The borkadrac's thumping gets closer. With a final tug, you pull the cloak free. You hear a loud ripping sound, and you're sure that somewhere your Nana must know you've torn the cloak she sewed for you. Of course, you tell yourself, she'll be more than happy that you're alive to be scolded rather than in some borkadrac's belly for lunch.

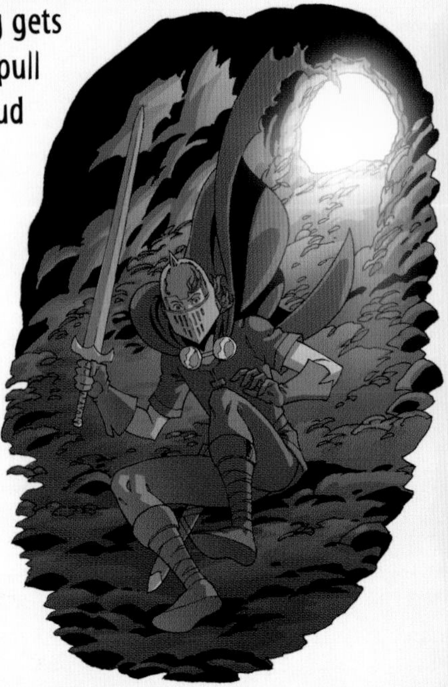

You tumble down a slight incline of silt and gravel while the borkadrac howls in frustration. It's too big to follow you.

At the bottom of the slope, you pull yourself to a sitting position and let your eyes adjust to the dark. After a few seconds, you notice an opening further down the tunnel.

You look more closely. The opening looks more like a real doorway than another cave tunnel. And wait – is that a torch in a bracket beside it? Maybe your luck is changing.

GO ON TO THE NEXT PAGE.

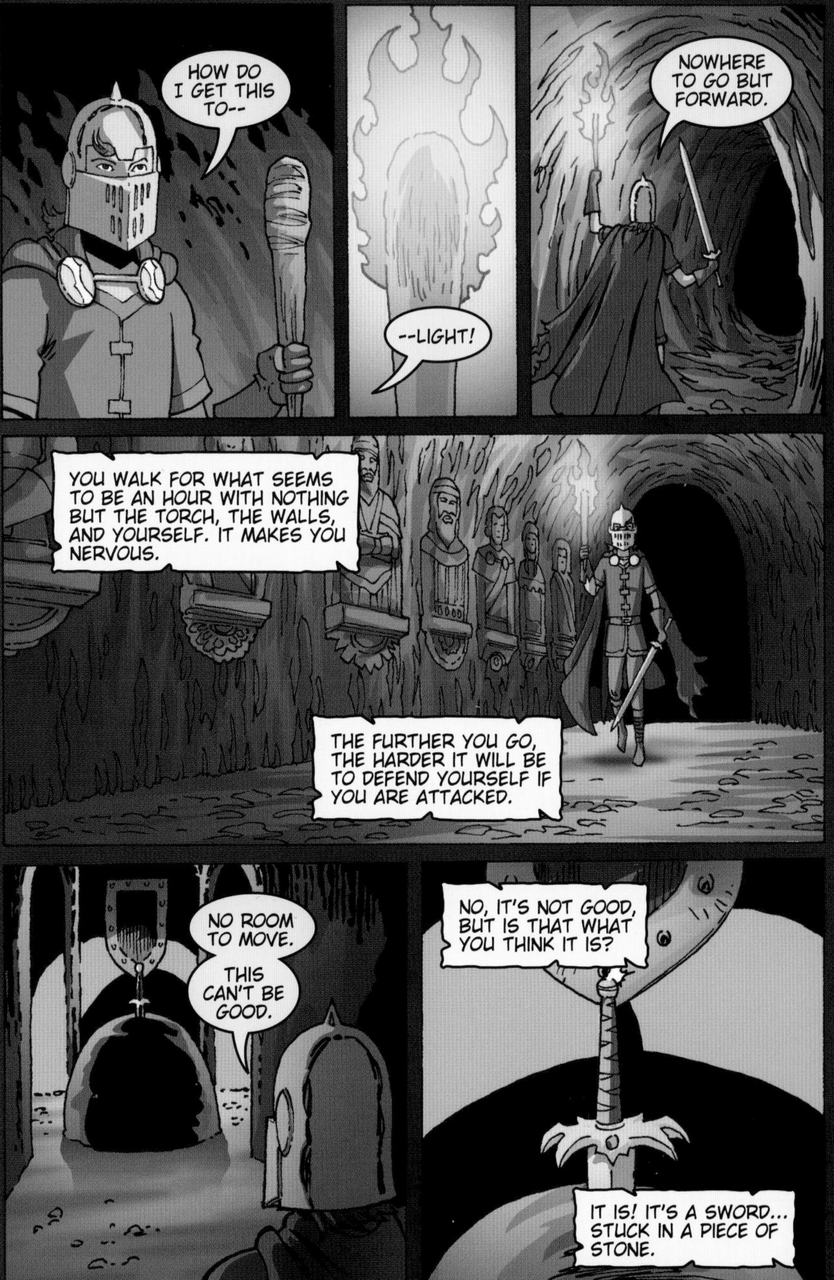
HOW DO I GET THIS TO--
--LIGHT!
NOWHERE TO GO BUT FORWARD.
YOU WALK FOR WHAT SEEMS TO BE AN HOUR WITH NOTHING BUT THE TORCH, THE WALLS, AND YOURSELF. IT MAKES YOU NERVOUS.
THE FURTHER YOU GO, THE HARDER IT WILL BE TO DEFEND YOURSELF IF YOU ARE ATTACKED.
NO ROOM TO MOVE.
THIS CAN'T BE GOOD.
NO, IT'S NOT GOOD, BUT IS THAT WHAT YOU THINK IT IS?
IT IS! IT'S A SWORD... STUCK IN A PIECE OF STONE.

You pull the sword. It's light, easy to swing.
The shield is just as light and decorated with a
single white stripe down the middle.

WILL YOU

carry your discoveries...

...to the left?
TURN TO PAGE 66.

...to the right?
TURN TO PAGE 111.

You look up into the golden eyes of the dragon Gartrugh. 'When I started out, I just wanted to be a famous hero.'

'Is that what you still want?' Gartrugh bends his neck and comes closer to you.

'I think so.' You stop for a second and purse your lips. 'But I don't know where to start.'

Gartrugh gestures with his wings towards the treasure in the rooms. 'Why, here. You will be the hero of Mount Fate. You will right wrongs and help those in need. My sons will help you.' Gartrugh points at himself with one claw. 'I will help you learn magic and other skills.'

You turn to look at Wizard Uchawi and the Lady of the Mount. 'What about them?'

'The wizard will be allowed to do what he wishes. The Lady will stay because she is doing what she does. But what will *you* do?'

GO ON TO THE NEXT PAGE.

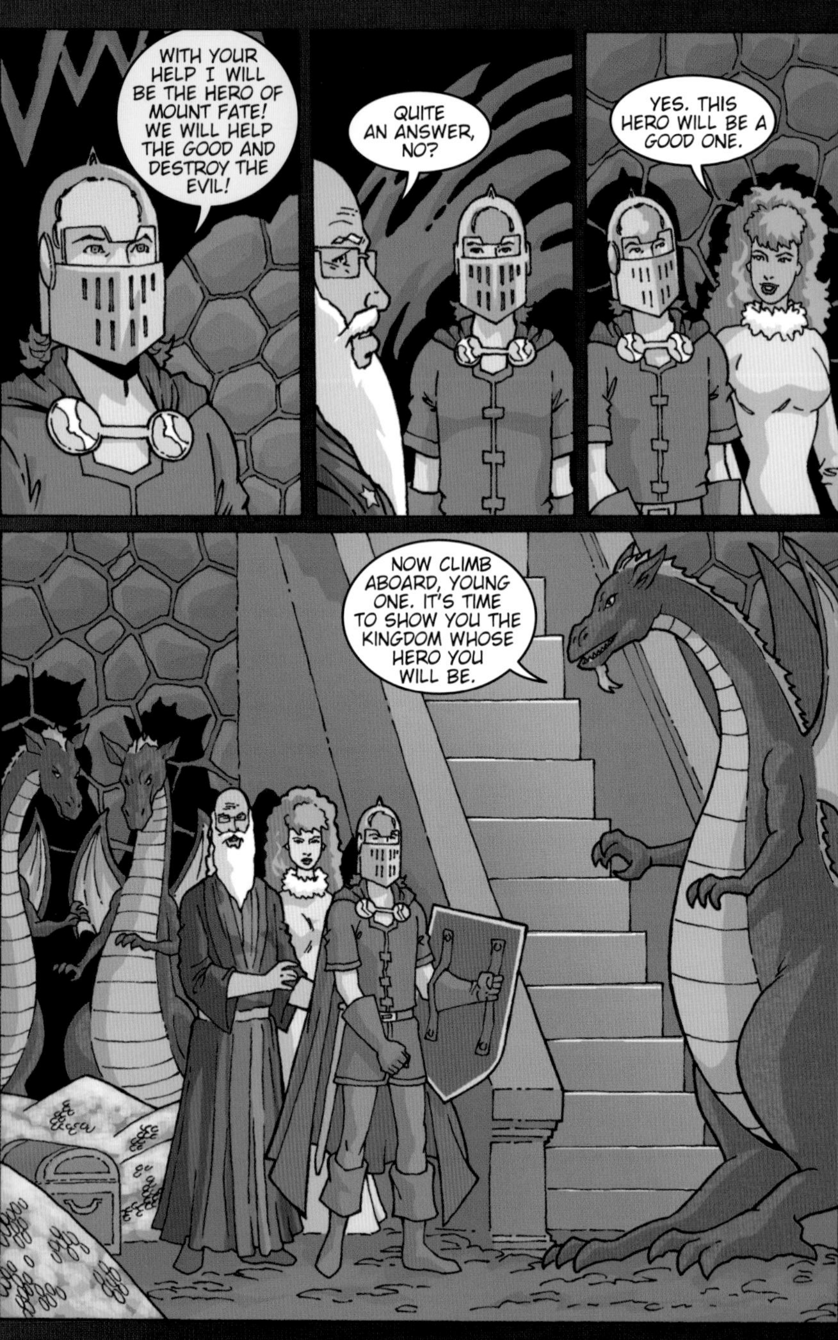
WITH YOUR HELP I WILL BE THE HERO OF MOUNT FATE! WE WILL HELP THE GOOD AND DESTROY THE EVIL!
QUITE AN ANSWER, NO?
YES. THIS HERO WILL BE A GOOD ONE.
NOW CLIMB ABOARD, YOUNG ONE. IT'S TIME TO SHOW YOU THE KINGDOM WHOSE HERO YOU WILL BE.

TURN TO PAGE 34.

The tunnel is damp but dry. Your fingertips touch the rough surface of the carved stone walls. They look like bricks. But somebody — probably somebodies — carved the stone to make it look so.

A faint tickle of breeze pushes you from behind, urging you on. The air smells faintly dusty, like a storeroom. Maybe you should turn around and go back and ...

Wait. A glint of light catches your eye. Something shiny, but not another light. Maybe a reflection? There must be something up ahead, something valuable.

TURN TO PAGE 91.

The torches go out, but Wizard Uchawi's magic wand sprouts a light. 'You lead the way,' he says.

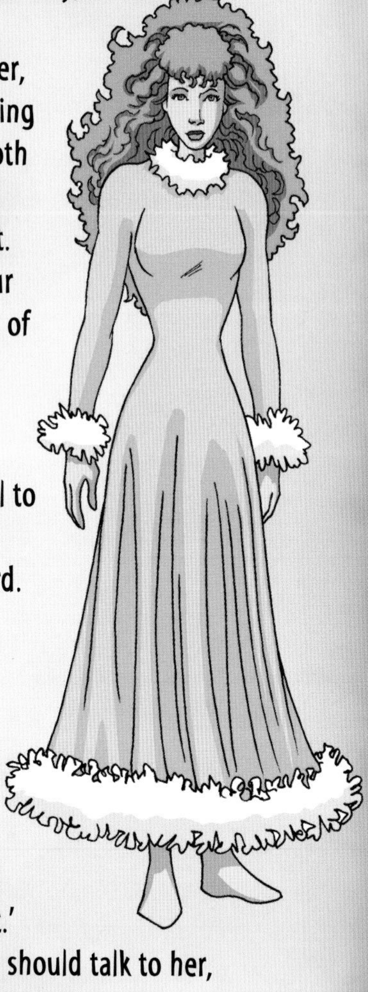

You walk for what seems forever, turning left and right in the twisting hall. The walls change from smooth to bricked to rough, then back to smooth again. It's strangely silent. The only sounds you hear are your breathing and the *clunkety-clunk* of Wizard Uchawi's possessions bouncing about.

'I think we're going in circles,' you say as you lean against a wall to catch your breath.

'I don't think so,' says the wizard. He points ahead with his wand.

'Libbety, lobbity, led,
Light, show us what's ahead.'

The globe grows bigger, then shoots a beam of light. Fifteen metres away, a lady dressed in a pink gown glitters.

'Hmmm, the Lady of the Mount.' Wizard Uchawi smiles. 'I think we should talk to her, don't you?'

You nod, not knowing what else to say.

GO ON TO THE NEXT PAGE.

The Lady smiles as you approach. Wizard Uchawi kneels and nudges you to do so as well.

'Adventurers, to save the mountain, I offer you a choice and a reward. You may face the dragon, you may face the genie, or you may face the ooze.'

WILL YOU CHOOSE...

...the dragon?
TURN TO PAGE 31.

...the ooze?
TURN TO PAGE 45.

...the genie?
TURN TO PAGE 82.

SHOOOOSH

WHOA!

SLAMM!

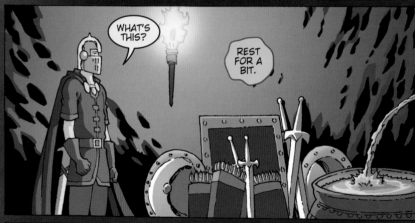

WHAT'S THIS?

REST FOR A BIT.

WHO'S THERE!

SHOW YOURSELF!

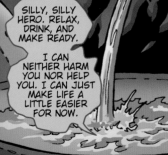

SILLY, SILLY HERO. RELAX, DRINK, AND MAKE READY.

I CAN NEITHER HARM YOU NOR HELP YOU. I CAN JUST MAKE LIFE A LITTLE EASIER FOR NOW.

The voice is a bit gurgly. 'I am a water sprite, hero, and I help those who enter this little room. High King Elodorat had it carved hundreds of years ago, when he fought the dragons. It's been years since anyone visited. Are you a soldier of the new High King?'

'No,' you answer. 'I'm on an adventure. I just escaped the borkadrac.'

'A borkadrac? My, those are nasty creatures. They never wash either. Did you know that? It's gone now, though. I can tell. Have a drink,' the sprite continues. 'It will help.'

You relax and take a gulp. The water is so cold, your head aches. But the sprite is right — it feels good.

'Can I take any of these?' you ask as you point at the arms.

'You can, but only one.'

You take a shield. It would have been helpful against the borkadrac.

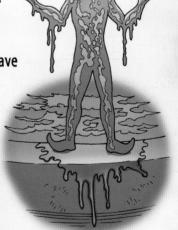

GO ON TO THE NEXT PAGE.

As the sprite speaks, you notice a tunnel leading out of the room. A magic torch lights the way.

WILL YOU...

...leave the room and head down the mountain?

TURN TO PAGE 78.

...go into the tunnel?

TURN TO PAGE 59.

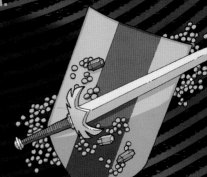

You have the lamp in your hands, but you don't know what to do with it. You've heard stories of rubbing a genie's lamp to command him, but they were just that – stories. The wizard will know what to do.

You reach back and throw the lamp towards Wizard Uchawi.

It arcs through the air, its polished surface glinting in the cavern's light. As the lamp leaves your hands, the genie bursts free!

'Nooo!' yells Wizard Uchawi.

'Yes!' booms the genie.

The room crackles with energy and you shut your eyes.

The air goes warm and it grows hard to breathe. You reach out and touch glass. When you open your eyes, you see you're in a small glass room. You pound on the glass, but it's unbreakable. You look left, right, up and down. All around you are others just like you. People who thought they would be heroes.

Instead, they are stuck here, collected like dolls in the genie's cavern.

THE END

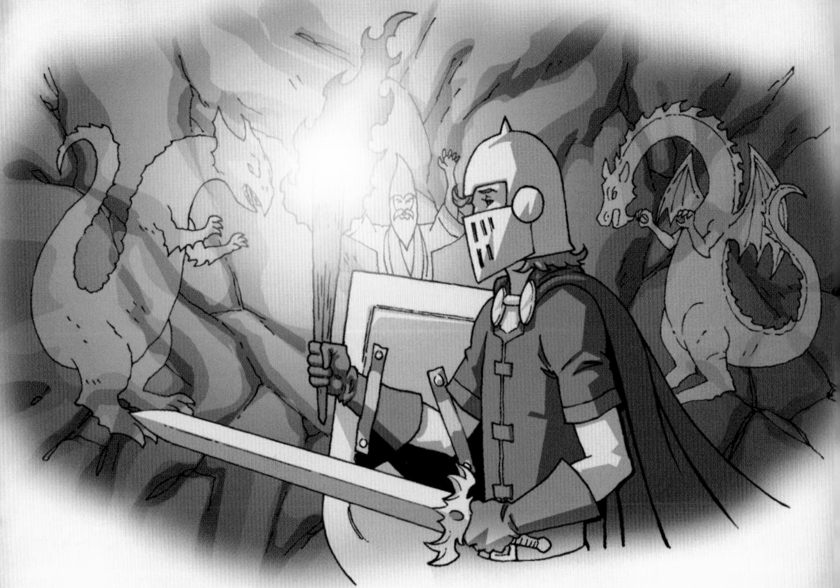

You turn to the left, gripping the sword. You couldn't hide your grin even if you tried. Your only regret is that you have no one to show this sword to. It feels like a part of you, swinging easily, not the slightest balance problem or awkwardness. Maybe it's magic.

The hall is remarkably silent. You can hear your own heartbeat as you walk forwards. Your footsteps echo away. Even the sound of your sword's scabbard slapping against you is loud. If any enemies are about down here, they'll hear you coming long before you know they're around.

That is not a comforting thought.

GO ON TO THE NEXT PAGE.

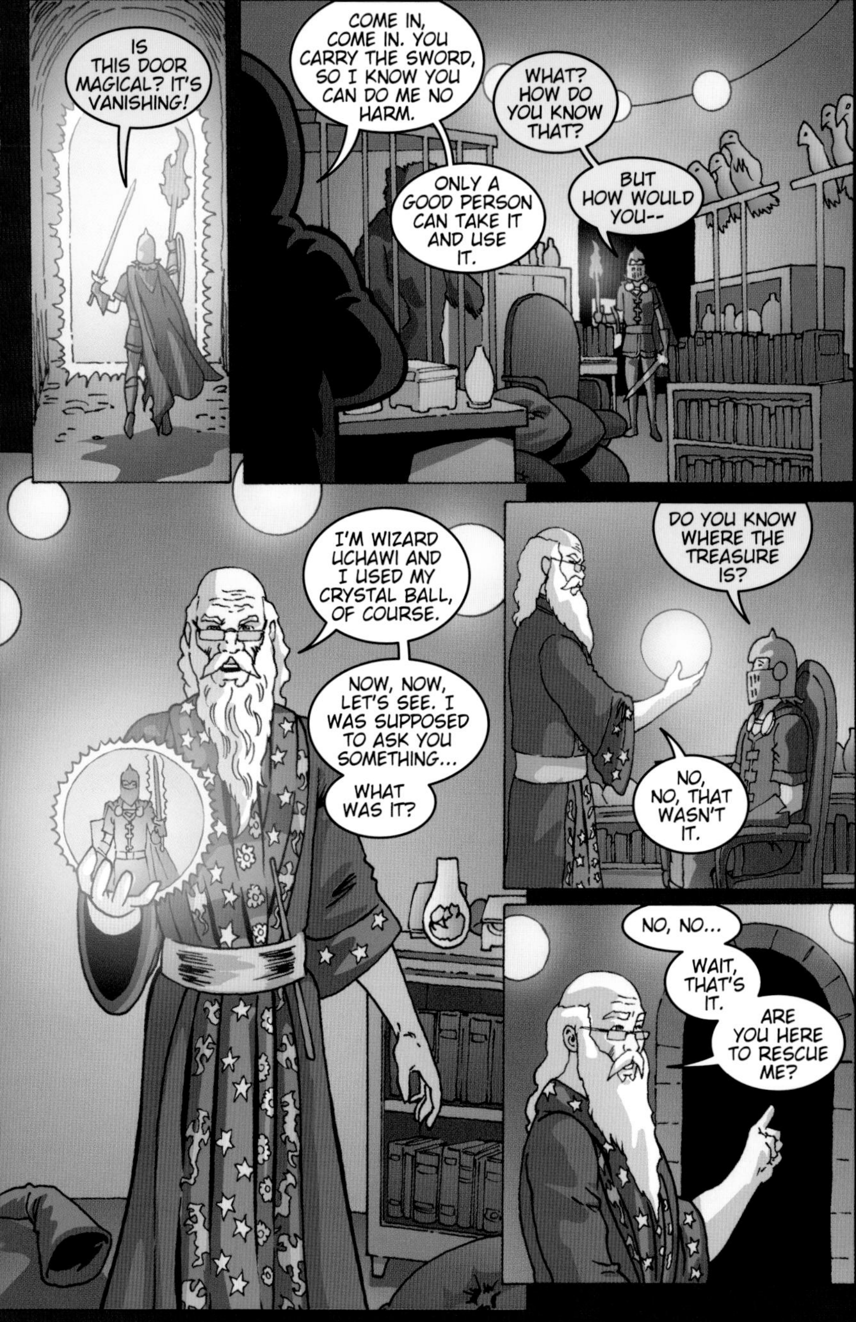
IS THIS DOOR MAGICAL? IT'S VANISHING!
COME IN, COME IN. YOU CARRY THE SWORD, SO I KNOW YOU CAN DO ME NO HARM.
ONLY A GOOD PERSON CAN TAKE IT AND USE IT.
WHAT? HOW DO YOU KNOW THAT?
BUT HOW WOULD YOU--
I'M WIZARD UCHAWI AND I USED MY CRYSTAL BALL, OF COURSE.
NOW, NOW, LET'S SEE. I WAS SUPPOSED TO ASK YOU SOMETHING...
WHAT WAS IT?
DO YOU KNOW WHERE THE TREASURE IS?
NO, NO, THAT WASN'T IT.
NO, NO...
WAIT, THAT'S IT.
ARE YOU HERE TO RESCUE ME?

GO ON TO THE NEXT PAGE.

'Well? Are you going to help me or not? If so, I have more packing to do and if not, then I'd rather stop packing, if you don't mind,' says the wizard as he looks over his spectacles at you.

WILL YOU...

...stall for time by saying you don't know if you can help?

TURN TO PAGE 16.

...say no?

TURN TO PAGE 28.

...say yes?

TURN TO PAGE 102.

At first you slide slowly down the slimy tunnel, but you build up speed. Zooming from side to side, you become covered in slime. Your sword tumbles free, as does the torch.

Suddenly, you feel nothing beneath you. Then you hit hard ground. You tumble head over heels, finally stopping in a pile of muck, sharp sticks, and stones.

You shake your head. Your eyes adjust to the darkness. Your torch lies a good distance away, still flaming, lighting the wall. Something is written there – and there's someone sitting there, too!

'Hello!' you shout as you make your way towards the torch.

Then you see. The someone isn't anyone, at least not anyone alive. It's a skeleton.

You realise the sticks on the ground aren't sticks, but bones. The room is full of skeletons.

The writing on the wall? 'NO ESCAPE' is all it says. And it's right.

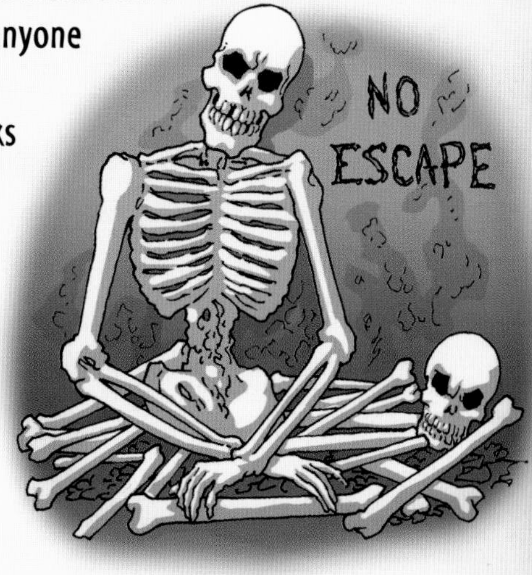
NO
ESCAPE

THE END

The thunderous roar of the fireball makes your ears ring. You pull the shield up over your head and hope it will be enough.

Too late, you realise this was the wrong choice.

The fireball burns thoroughly, so hot that it leaves nothing in its wake. The hall goes dark and silent. No one will ever know you were here.

THE END

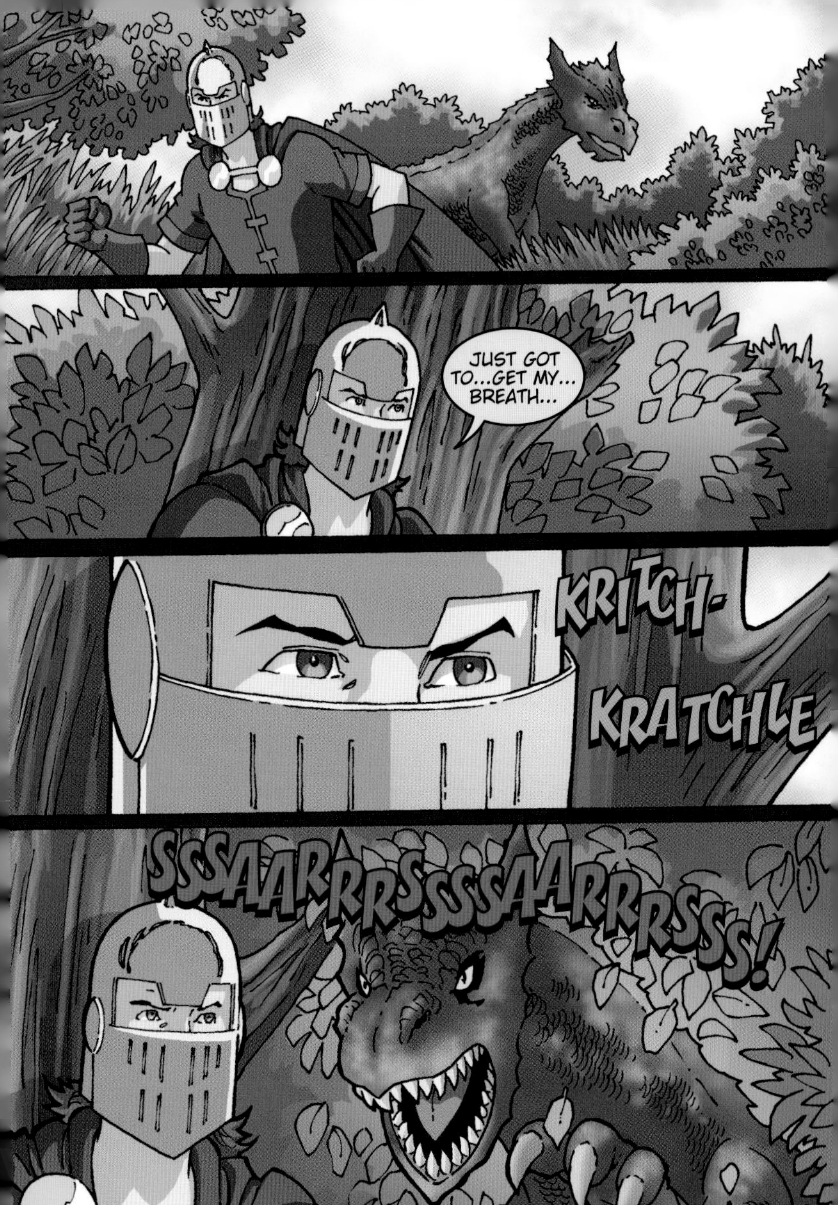
JUST GOT TO...GET MY... BREATH...
KRITCH-
KRATCHLE
SSSAARRRSSSSAARRRSSS!

It's right there behind you. The borkadrac's hot, steamy breath makes you want to be sick. You twist aside, pulling at the branches of the bushes around you.

You want to scream, but there's no time. You force your way through the bushes, letting the branches go. They flap by you, slapping the monster. Maybe they'll hurt it enough to help you get away.

You don't know where you're going. You just run. You push bushes out of the way, snap branches and stomp on dead twigs. You're too noisy. You don't have a chance of the borkadrac not catching you. Your only hope is to keep running. Running fast. Running far.

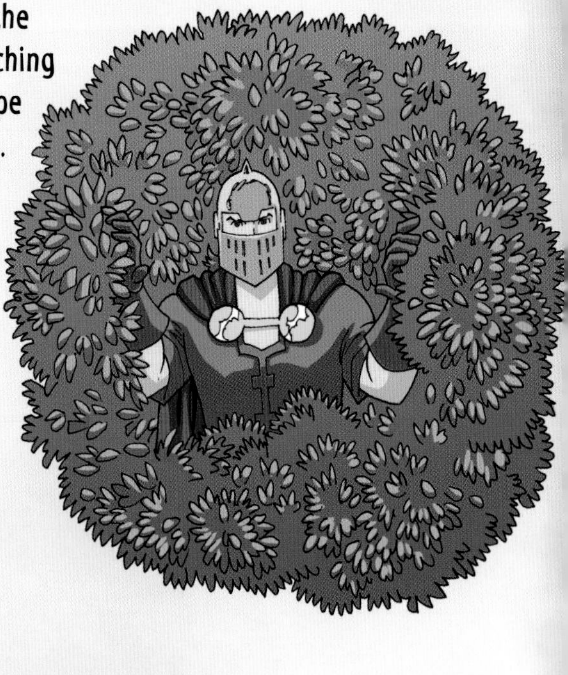

GO ON TO THE NEXT PAGE.

Before you is a stony path that leads up the mountain. To the right is a narrow path, probably used by mountain goats, that leads down.

Hurry, hurry, if you take too long you're going to be borkadrac feed!

WILL YOU...

...go down the mountain?
TURN TO PAGE 22.

...go up the mountain?
TURN TO PAGE 98.

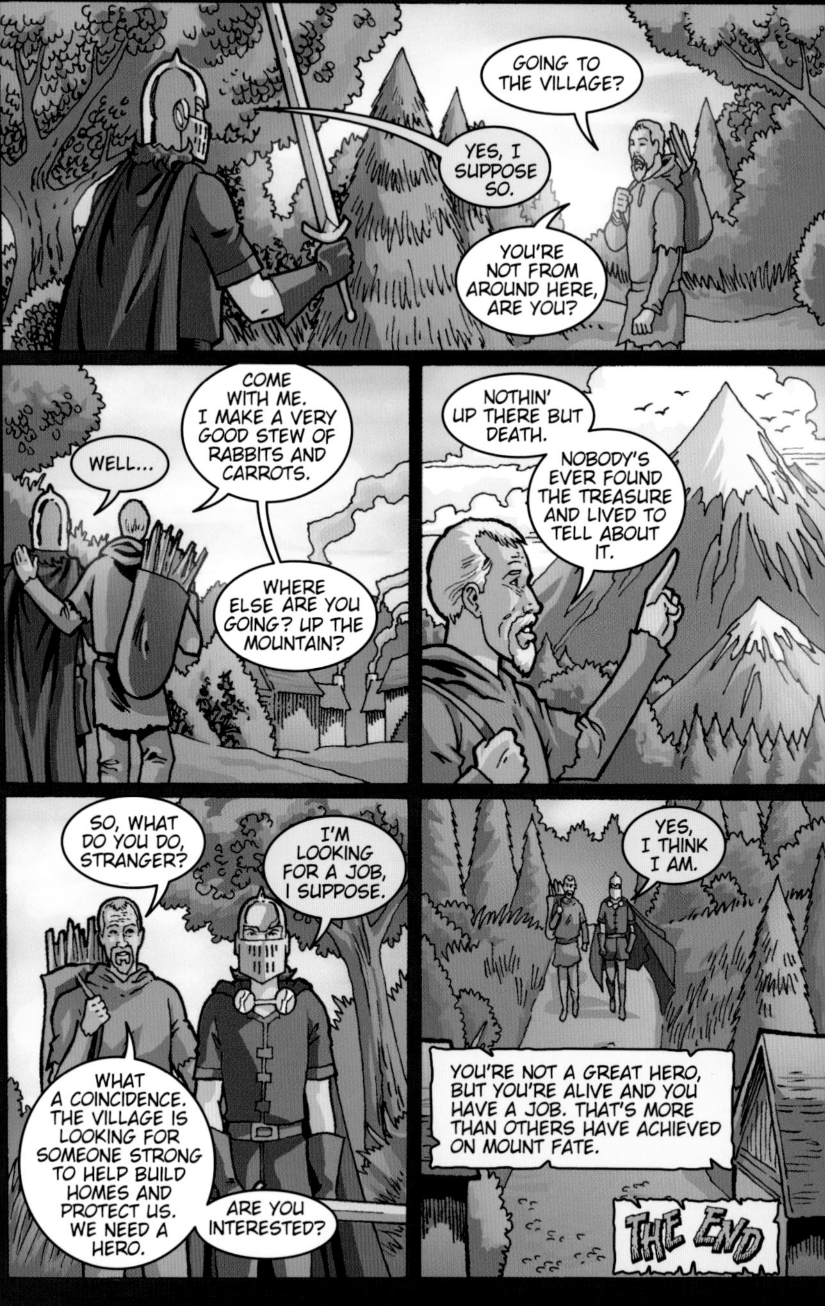
GOING TO THE VILLAGE?
YES, I SUPPOSE SO.
YOU'RE NOT FROM AROUND HERE, ARE YOU?
WELL...
COME WITH ME. I MAKE A VERY GOOD STEW OF RABBITS AND CARROTS.
WHERE ELSE ARE YOU GOING? UP THE MOUNTAIN?
NOTHIN' UP THERE BUT DEATH.
NOBODY'S EVER FOUND THE TREASURE AND LIVED TO TELL ABOUT IT.
SO, WHAT DO YOU DO, STRANGER?
I'M LOOKING FOR A JOB, I SUPPOSE.
WHAT A COINCIDENCE. THE VILLAGE IS LOOKING FOR SOMEONE STRONG TO HELP BUILD HOMES AND PROTECT US. WE NEED A HERO.
ARE YOU INTERESTED?
YES, I THINK I AM.
YOU'RE NOT A GREAT HERO, BUT YOU'RE ALIVE AND YOU HAVE A JOB. THAT'S MORE THAN OTHERS HAVE ACHIEVED ON MOUNT FATE.
THE END

You scamper backwards, your head swivelling between the door and the soldiers. They keep clumping towards you, their heavy steps echoing in the hallway. Their pounding weight makes vibrations so strong that you feel like the whole hallway could cave in.

You reach for the door handle, but first you check the soldiers again. You've got enough time to look away...for a moment.

You pull on the handle, but the door doesn't budge.

You push on the handle, but the door still doesn't budge.

Locked! You groan.

GO ON TO THE NEXT PAGE.

Of all the rotten luck. There's no time to think. You turn to face the soldiers.

Wait. The sword is magic. It cuts through stone...What else does it cut through?

WILL YOU...

...stand and fight the soldiers with your magic sword and shield?

TURN TO PAGE 33.

...strike the door with your magic sword?

TURN TO PAGE 87.

You jump up and catch hold of the rope. You get both hands on it and wrap it around each wrist. It feels a bit tight, but looking down, you realise you have no option but to hold on or to fall hundreds of metres onto the rocks below.

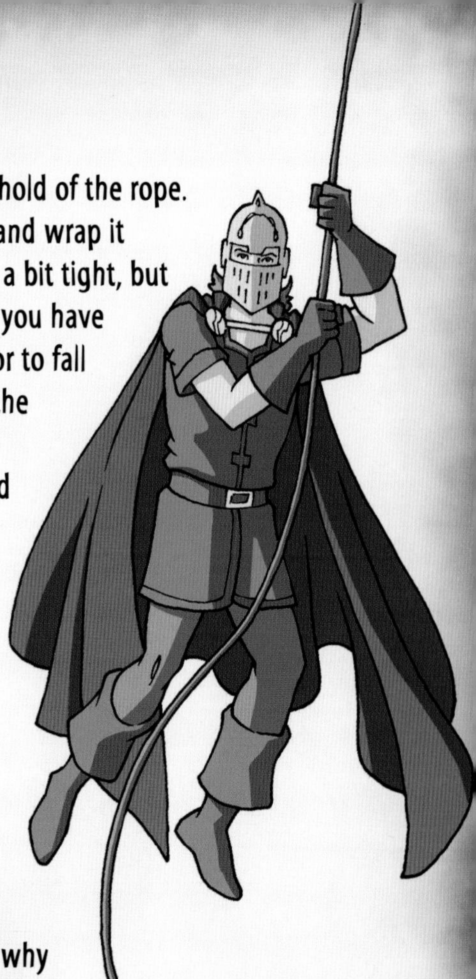

Wizard Uchawi turns and smiles. 'I thought you were pretty clever.' He gestures with his hand, and the rope softens, but it still holds you securely. 'I'll be needing a servant in River City and I think you'll prove to be the one.'

A servant! No! You were going to be a hero. That's why Alaric taught you all those fighting skills.

You can't let go of the rope – it's holding you snugly. You doubt it'll let go when you land, either.

Servant? Not likely. You're going to be a slave.

THE END

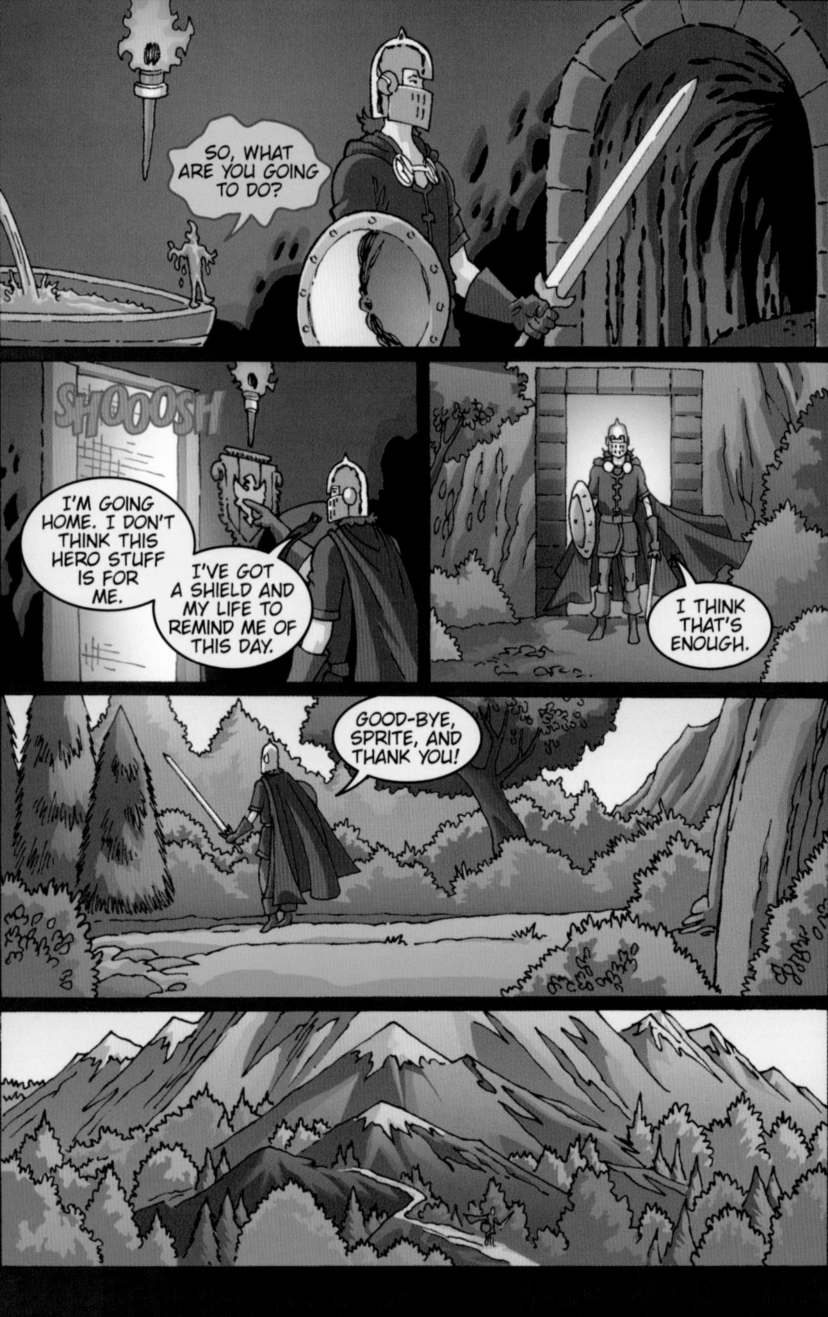
SO, WHAT ARE YOU GOING TO DO?
SHOOOSH
I'M GOING HOME. I DON'T THINK THIS HERO STUFF IS FOR ME.
I'VE GOT A SHIELD AND MY LIFE TO REMIND ME OF THIS DAY.
I THINK THAT'S ENOUGH.
GOOD-BYE, SPRITE, AND THANK YOU!

GO ON TO THE NEXT PAGE.

A simple life with no adventure is not a bad life. You will marry, have children and enjoy every day. You will rescue a starving dog, which you'll name Bounder. He'll go everywhere you go.

You'll also have the tale of how you fought a borkadrac, met a water sprite and found a shield. And later, when you're much older, your grandchildren will ask to hear it over and over again, to your delight.

THE END

You take the fight to the beast. If you're meant to be a hero, you'll earn it here on the side of Mount Fate. You swing your sword just as you were trained to do.

This beast will be your claim to fame. From its hide you will make boots that are like no others. People will speak your name in awe as they sing the song of your deeds.

But the beast steps backwards. It keeps itself just out of reach of your sword.

GO ON TO THE NEXT PAGE.

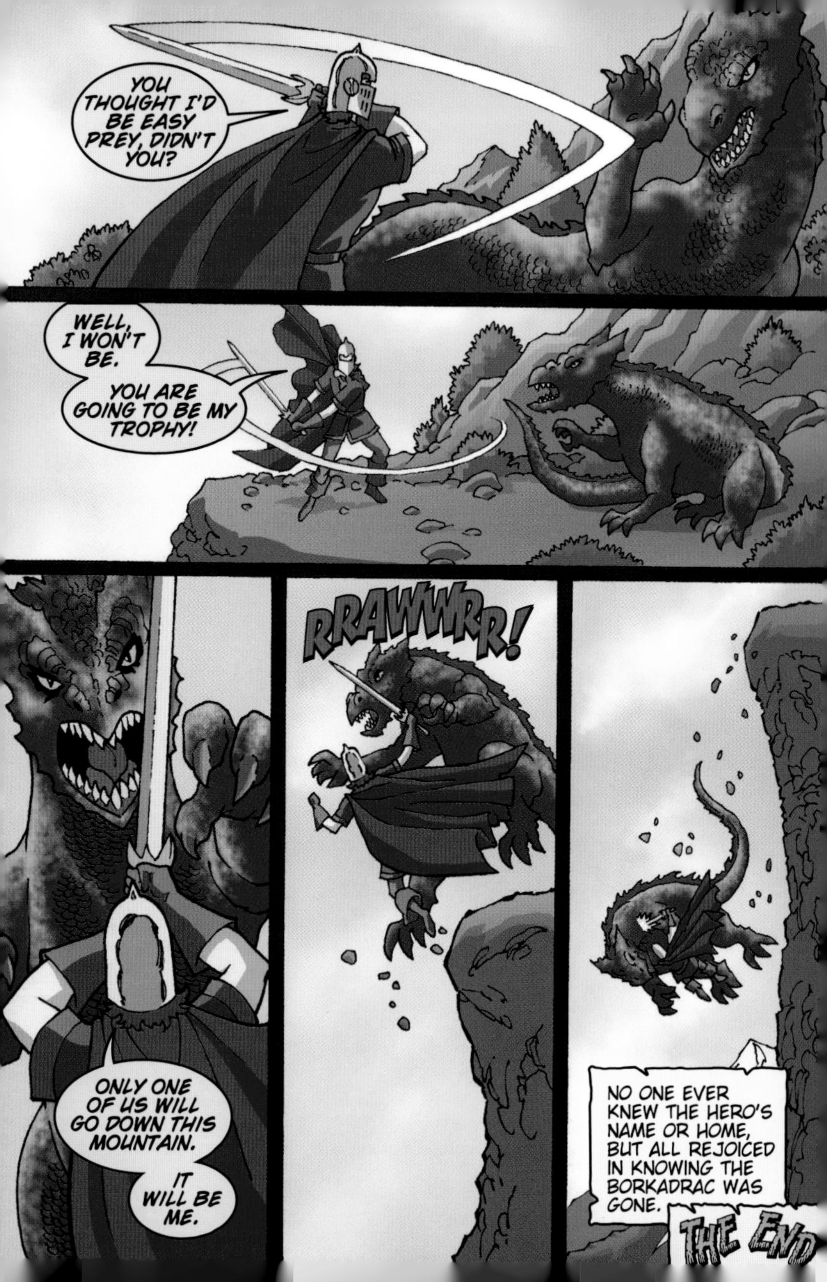
YOU THOUGHT I'D BE EASY PREY, DIDN'T YOU?
WELL, I WON'T BE.
YOU ARE GOING TO BE MY TROPHY!
ONLY ONE OF US WILL GO DOWN THIS MOUNTAIN.
IT WILL BE ME.
RRAWWRR!
NO ONE EVER KNEW THE HERO'S NAME OR HOME, BUT ALL REJOICED IN KNOWING THE BORKADRAC WAS GONE.
THE END

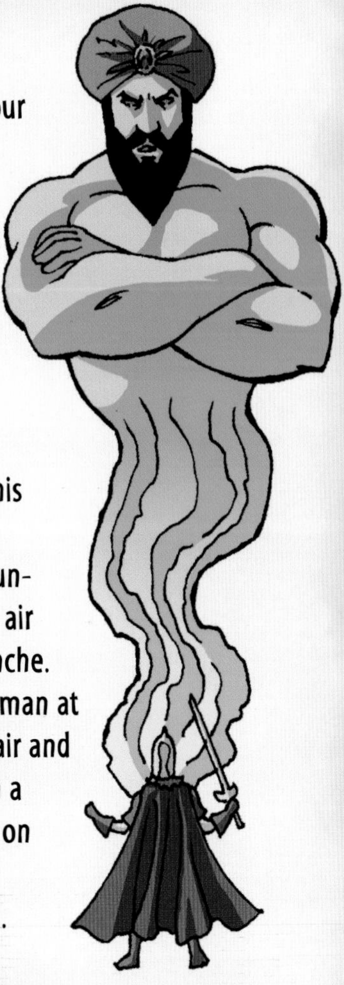

The Lady of the Mount touches your head. Everything goes blue.

You open your eyes to a sparkling pile of gold, sapphires, rubies, diamonds, shields, urns and much more. You mouth the word 'wow,' but no sound comes out.

'My, my. I am impressed.' Wizard Uchawi holds up a ruby the size of his palm.

'I do not think I am.' The voice thunders through the room, shaking the air and causing a pile of coins to avalanche.

You look up and see above you a man at least fifteen metres tall with long hair and a full beard. He wears a turban with a giant diamond clasp and gold rings on every finger.

You point at him with your sword. 'You must be the genie.'

The genie laughs and gestures to glass cages with heroes like you locked within. 'And you must be next.'

 GO ON TO THE NEXT PAGE.

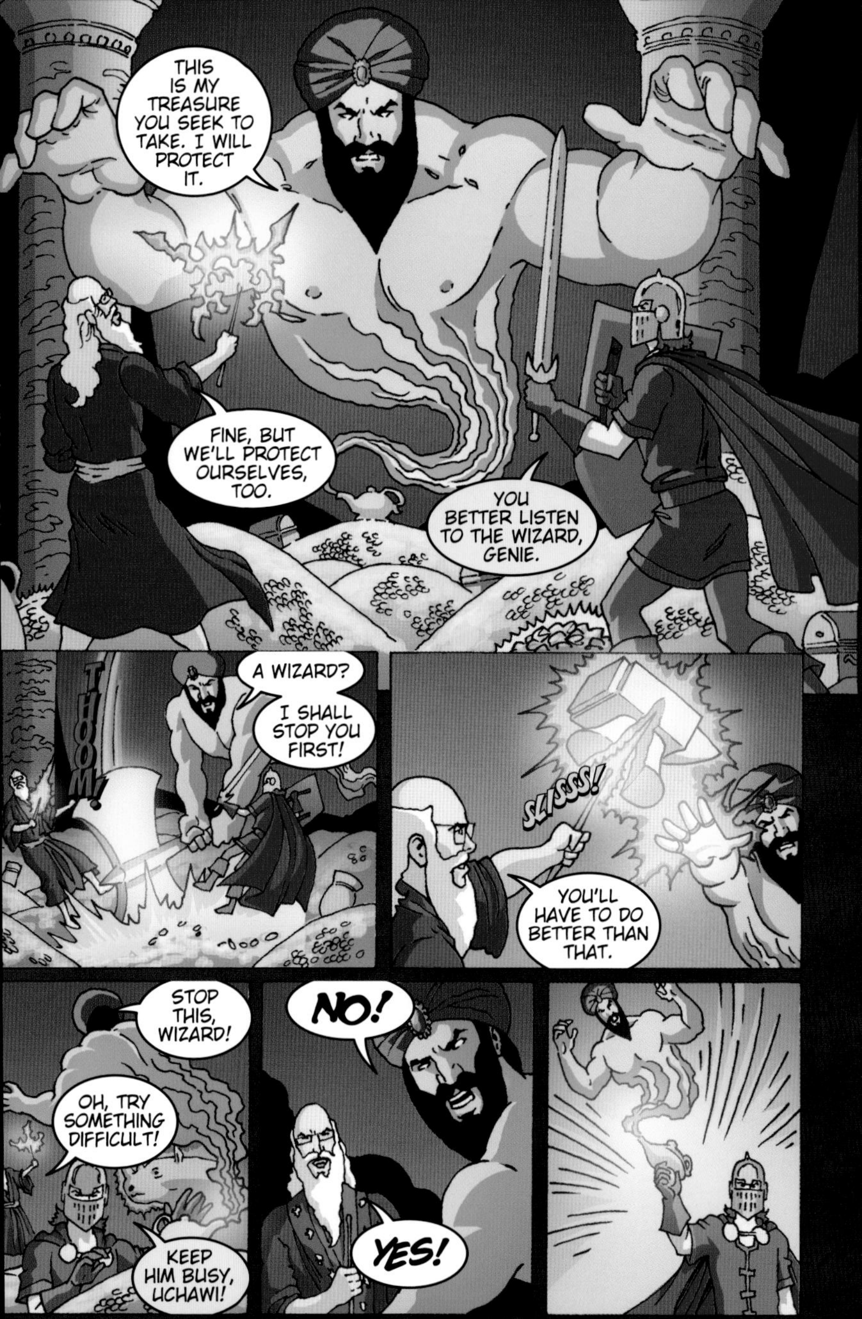

THIS IS MY TREASURE YOU SEEK TO TAKE. I WILL PROTECT IT.
FINE, BUT WE'LL PROTECT OURSELVES, TOO.
YOU BETTER LISTEN TO THE WIZARD, GENIE.
THOOM!
A WIZARD?
I SHALL STOP YOU FIRST!
SLISSSS!
YOU'LL HAVE TO DO BETTER THAN THAT.
STOP THIS, WIZARD!
OH, TRY SOMETHING DIFFICULT!
KEEP HIM BUSY, UCHAWI!
NO!
YES!

GO ON TO THE NEXT PAGE.

You have the lamp. The genie is trapped. Now what?

WILL YOU...

...rub the lamp, hoping the genie will come out and do your bidding?

TURN TO PAGE 35.

...throw the lamp to Wizard Uchawi?

TURN TO PAGE 65.

No, you tell yourself, others have been here already. They would have taken whatever treasure was here. You reach up to place the torch back into the bracket. A giggle stops you. It sounds like fingernails scraping across a blackboard.

'Who's there?' you ask. More giggles. You feel goosebumps form all over your body. That giggle isn't a giggle at all. It's the sound of goblins talking.

Quick as a flash, you draw your sword. You grab your shield with your other hand. It only sounds like four or five. Nothing you can't handle.

GO ON TO THE NEXT PAGE.

You were wrong. There are quite a few more than four or five.

About ten times that many.

They close in on you, pressing hard. You try to swing your sword, but you can't because they're grabbing your arm. They even grab at your shield.

Before you know it, you're being dragged away along the tunnel. The goblins pull you down a passage you hadn't noticed, one where the breeze is quite strong. You realise you should have thought more about that tickling breeze you'd felt behind you. Too late now, though. You're going to spend the rest of your life as a goblin slave, carving tunnels in the mountains as your captors mine for their precious goblin rocks.

THE END

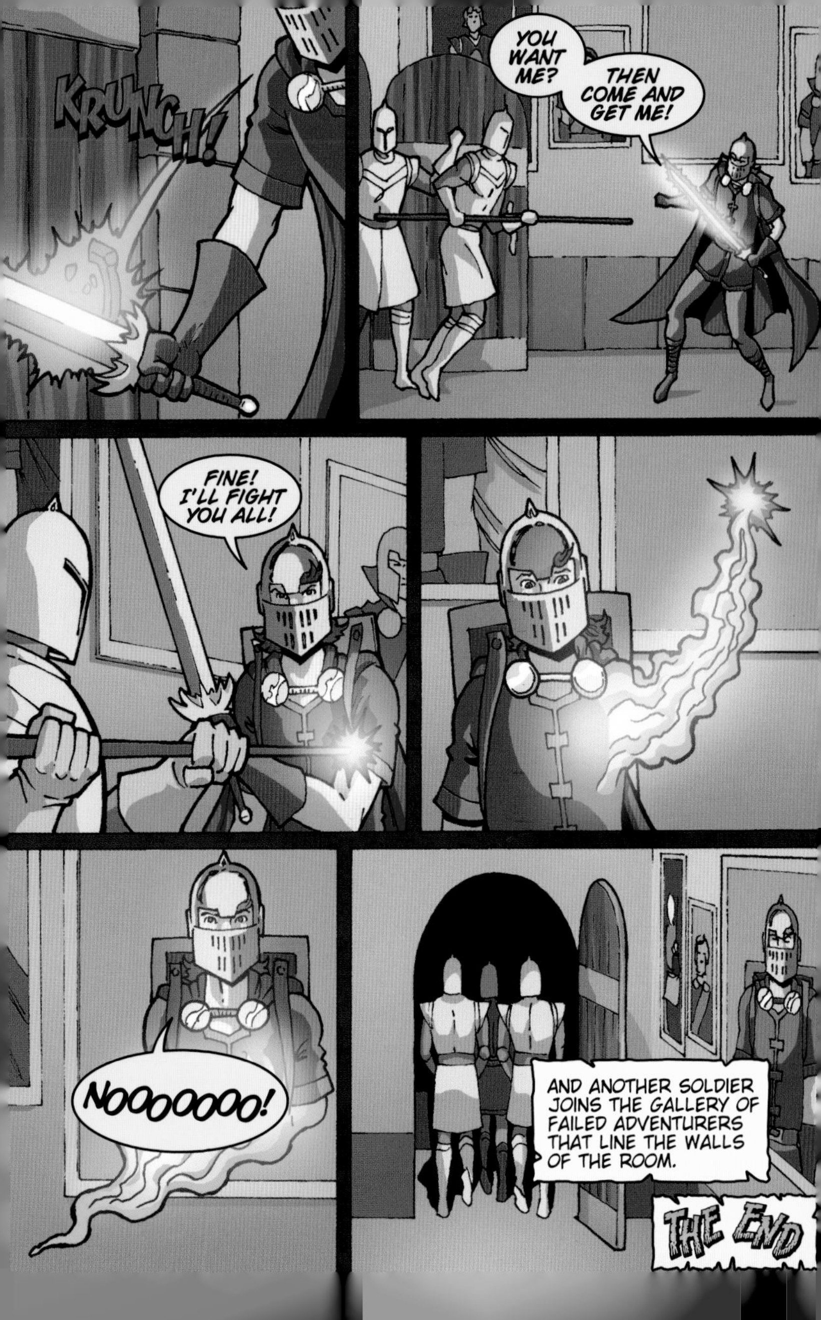
KRUNCH!
YOU WANT ME?
THEN COME AND GET ME!
FINE! I'LL FIGHT YOU ALL!
NOOOOOOO!
AND ANOTHER SOLDIER JOINS THE GALLERY OF FAILED ADVENTURERS THAT LINE THE WALLS OF THE ROOM.
THE END

You press the down arrow and the doors open to show a small, box-like room.

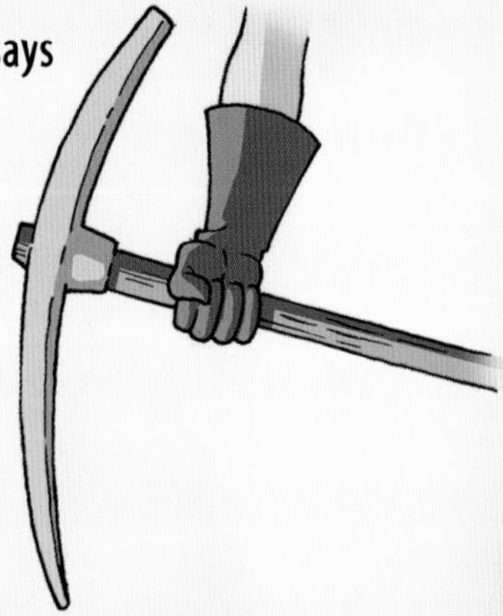

'This doesn't seem quite right,' says Wizard Uchawi. 'I wish my magic wand was working.'

You both step inside. The doors whoosh shut. Your legs go light, and you feel like you're moving downwards. Then the movement stops.

The door opens and a big beast covered with hair grabs you and hands you a pickaxe. Another one, just like him, does the same with Wizard Uchawi.

The beasts push you down a walkway and into a dark cave spotted with little torches. You see creatures of all types swinging pickaxes at the walls, pushing carts or carrying rocks.

The beast pushes you forwards. 'GET TO WORK, SLAVE!'

'How do we get out of here?' you whisper to Wizard Uchawi, but he just waves his broken wand .

'I don't think we do. I think we're here forever,' he says as a beast drags him away.

THE END

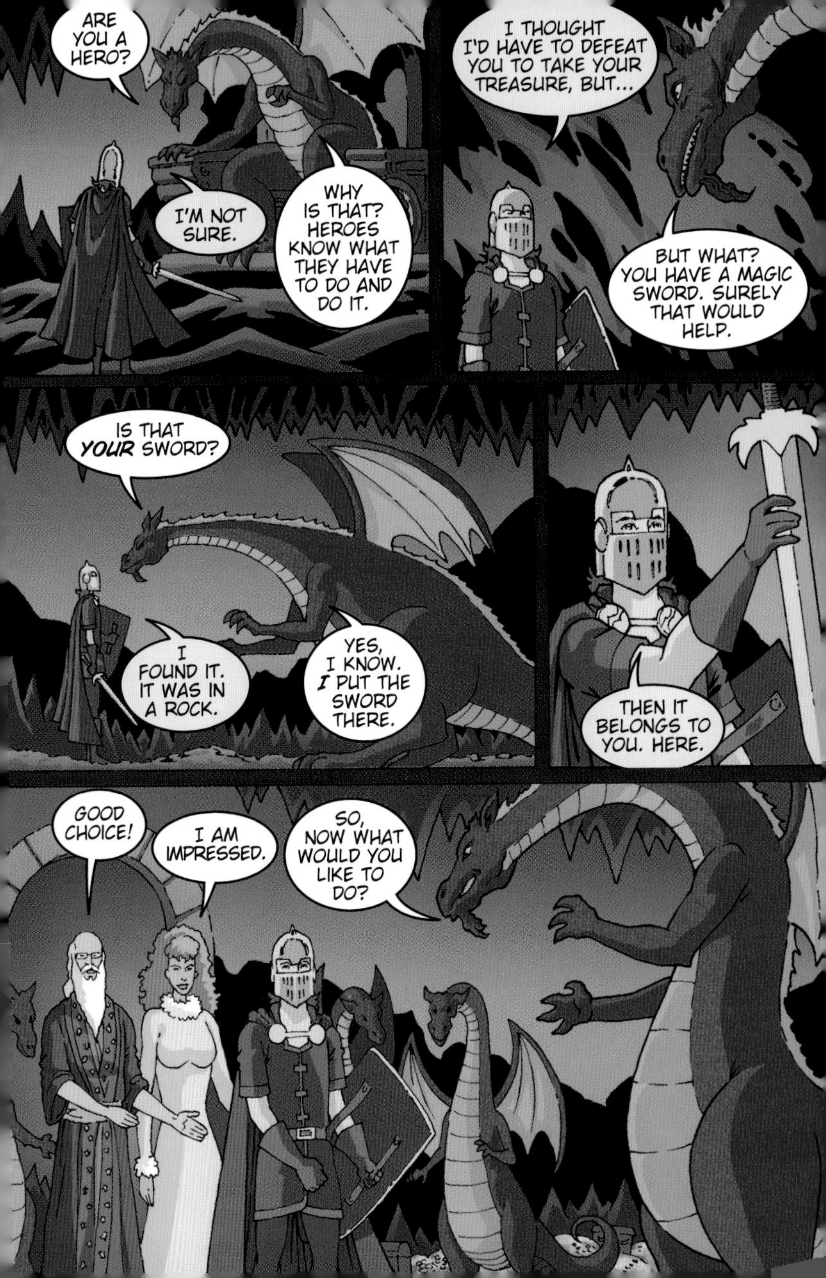
ARE YOU A HERO?
I'M NOT SURE.
WHY IS THAT? HEROES KNOW WHAT THEY HAVE TO DO AND DO IT.
I THOUGHT I'D HAVE TO DEFEAT YOU TO TAKE YOUR TREASURE, BUT...
BUT WHAT? YOU HAVE A MAGIC SWORD. SURELY THAT WOULD HELP.
IS THAT *YOUR* SWORD?
I FOUND IT. IT WAS IN A ROCK.
YES, I KNOW. *I* PUT THE SWORD THERE.
THEN IT BELONGS TO YOU. HERE.
GOOD CHOICE!
I AM IMPRESSED.
SO, NOW WHAT WOULD YOU LIKE TO DO?

Your feet slide a bit as you stand to fight, but the slick ground works in your favour, too. A soldier swings at you and misses. The force of his swing takes him too far and he slips on the slime. He slides down the tunnel, flailing silently.

You turn back – too slowly. The butt of an axe strikes your shoulder. It hurts. It burns.

You lift your hand. Your fingers won't bend! As you look at it, the soldiers stop attacking. Your hand is all smooth and waxy looking. Before your very eyes, it begins to drip.

You look down at your feet, but they're not there! They've melted away in a slimy mess.

Oh no. This hallway must be cursed. Any living thing – like you – turns to slime.

Time seems to come to a stop as you slowly melt. Your clothes and armour fall away and at last you are absorbed into the slime that is all that remains of those who came before you.

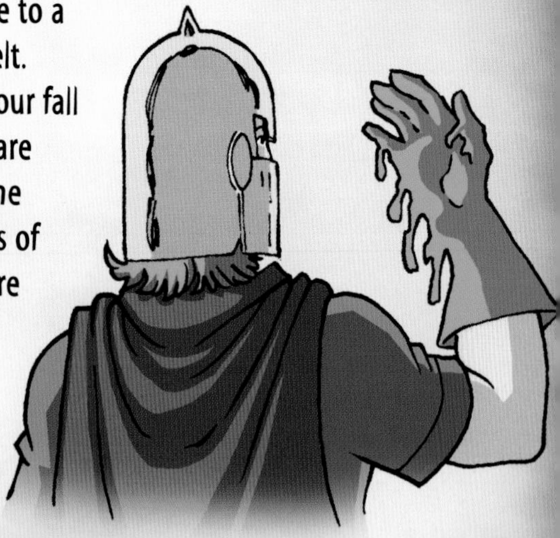

THE END

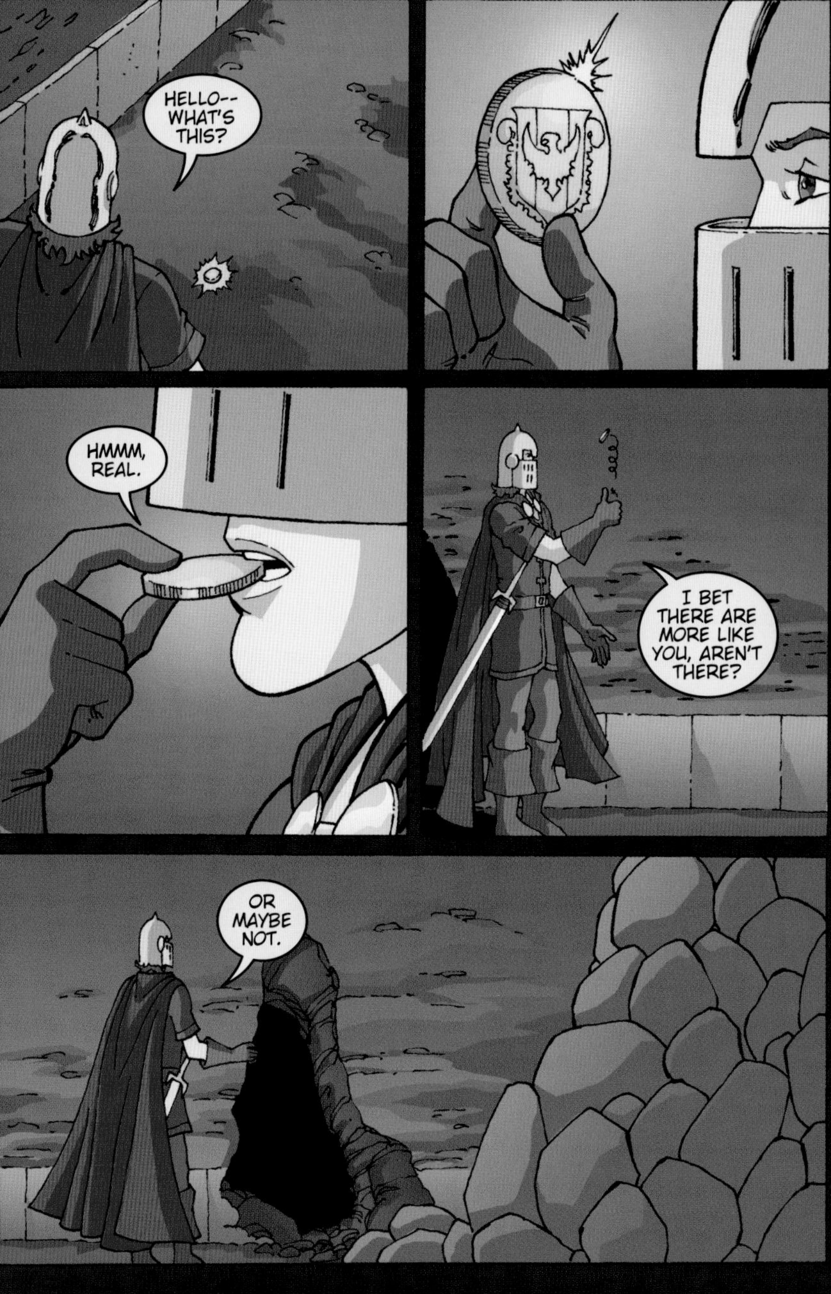
HELLO--
WHAT'S
THIS?
HMMM,
REAL.
I BET
THERE ARE
MORE LIKE
YOU, AREN'T
THERE?
OR
MAYBE
NOT.

GO ON TO THE NEXT PAGE.

You take down a torch from the wall and poke it into the hole. Cobwebs grab at you, but you brush them away. A tiny black beetle skitters into the darkness.

WILL YOU...

...go into the new tunnel?
TURN TO PAGE 50.

...turn around and go back?
TURN TO PAGE 85.

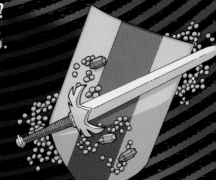

You turn and charge the army of little spiders. You stamp and you stomp and you slap and you swing, hitting spiders with every movement.

But for every ten you take down, at least ten more seem to fill their places. They're everywhere. Crawling on you arms, on your legs, across your chest, in your hair. And they bite.

You keep moving, but the bites start to sting. The spiders are inside your clothes, down your back, inside your boots.

You throw yourself against the walls, hoping to crush some. Your eyesight gets blurry. Your legs feel heavy, each step slower and slower, until you tumble down.

The spiders keep crawling over you, but you can't feel them anymore. There's no more pain as they begin to wrap you up in their silky webs, preparing to store you for a later feast for their colony.

THE END

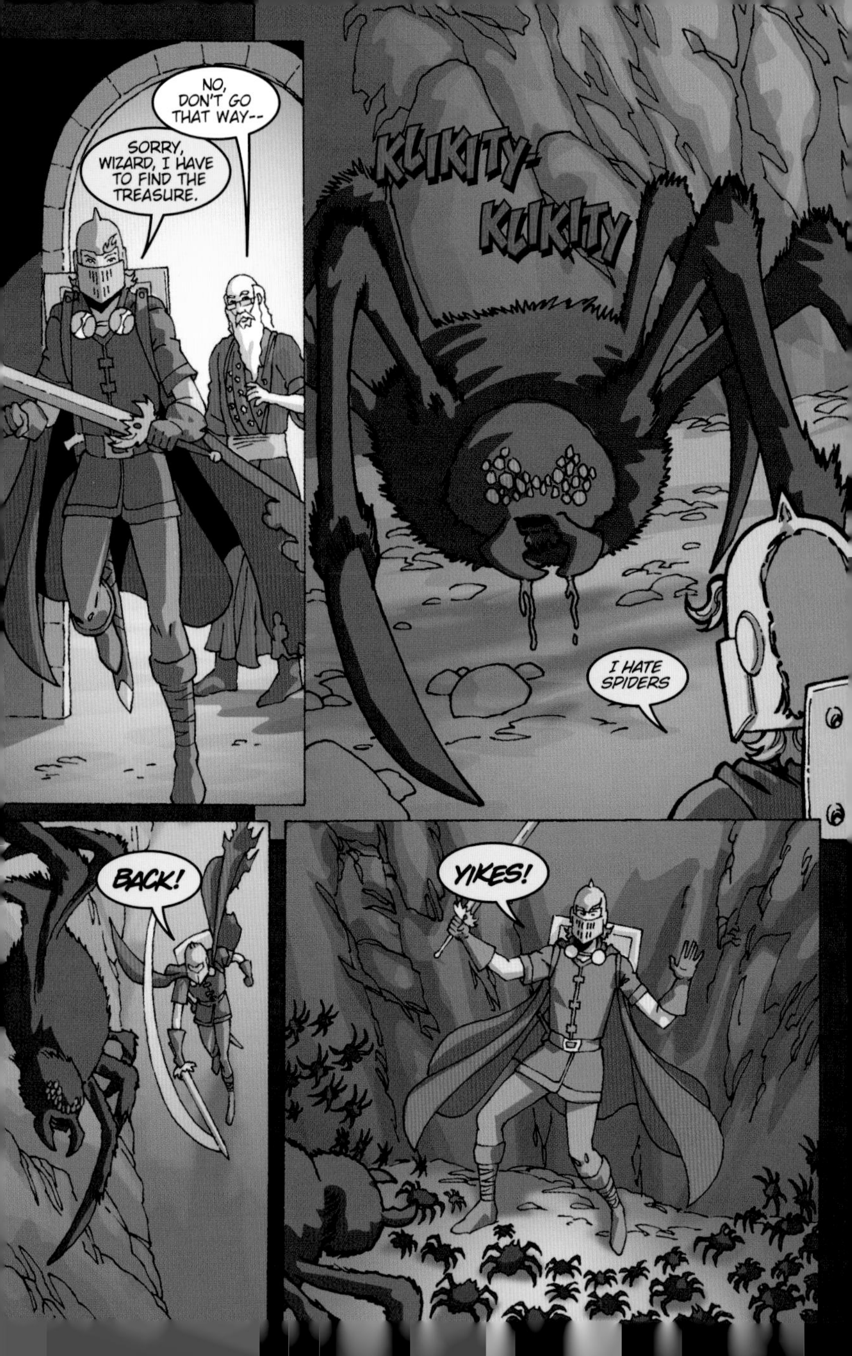
NO, DON'T GO THAT WAY--
SORRY, WIZARD, I HAVE TO FIND THE TREASURE.
KLIKITY-KLIKITY
I HATE SPIDERS
BACK!
YIKES!

You look down and then back at the rope. If you jump and miss, you'll plunge hundreds of metres to your death on the rocks below.

You go back to the staircase. You step onto the steps, but they're still turning upwards. You can't run down fast enough to make any progress. In fact, the staircase keeps throwing you off, like a small spinning catapult.

Next you look for a down arrow like the one you saw inside, but there's nothing. Just you and the turning stairs to keep you company.

You look around and realise you can see for many kilometres in all directions, but there's nobody to see you. You made it to the top of Mount Fate, but you have no treasure and no one even knows you got this far. Even worse, you will be stuck here at the top of the mountain… forever.

THE END

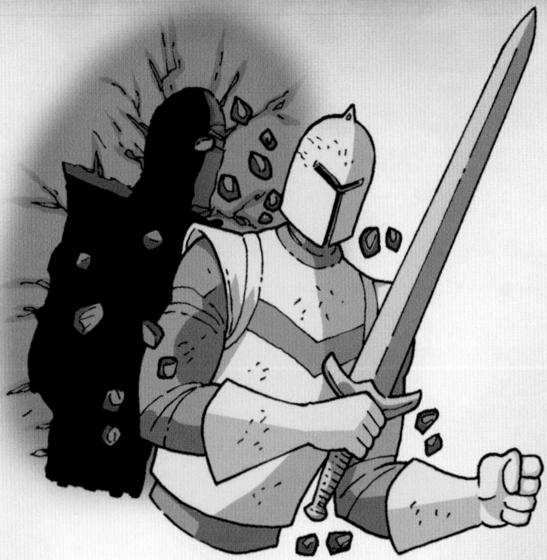

You parry attacks, occasionally striking one of the stone soldiers, but you can't keep this up forever. They don't seem to tire.

You, however, have been going non-stop since you woke up this morning. You're hungry, tired and thirsty. You need a rest, but you won't be getting one soon. The soldiers just keep on coming at you. Every sculpture you pass becomes another soldier. One replaces every one you defeat.

If you stop, you don't know what will happen to you, but if you continue, you can't be sure either.

As you shuffle backwards down the tunnel, you realise that the air is getting a bit cooler and a bit damper. The walls seem almost greasy from some sort of slime growing on them.

Your foot slides out from under you and you fall, sliding backwards.

GO ON TO THE NEXT PAGE.

You look up from the hard floor. The stone soldiers are still walking towards you, with more and more appearing behind them.

WILL YOU...

...pull yourself up to fight?
TURN TO PAGE 69.

...let yourself slide down the tunnel, knowing you can't beat the soldiers?
TURN TO PAGE 90.

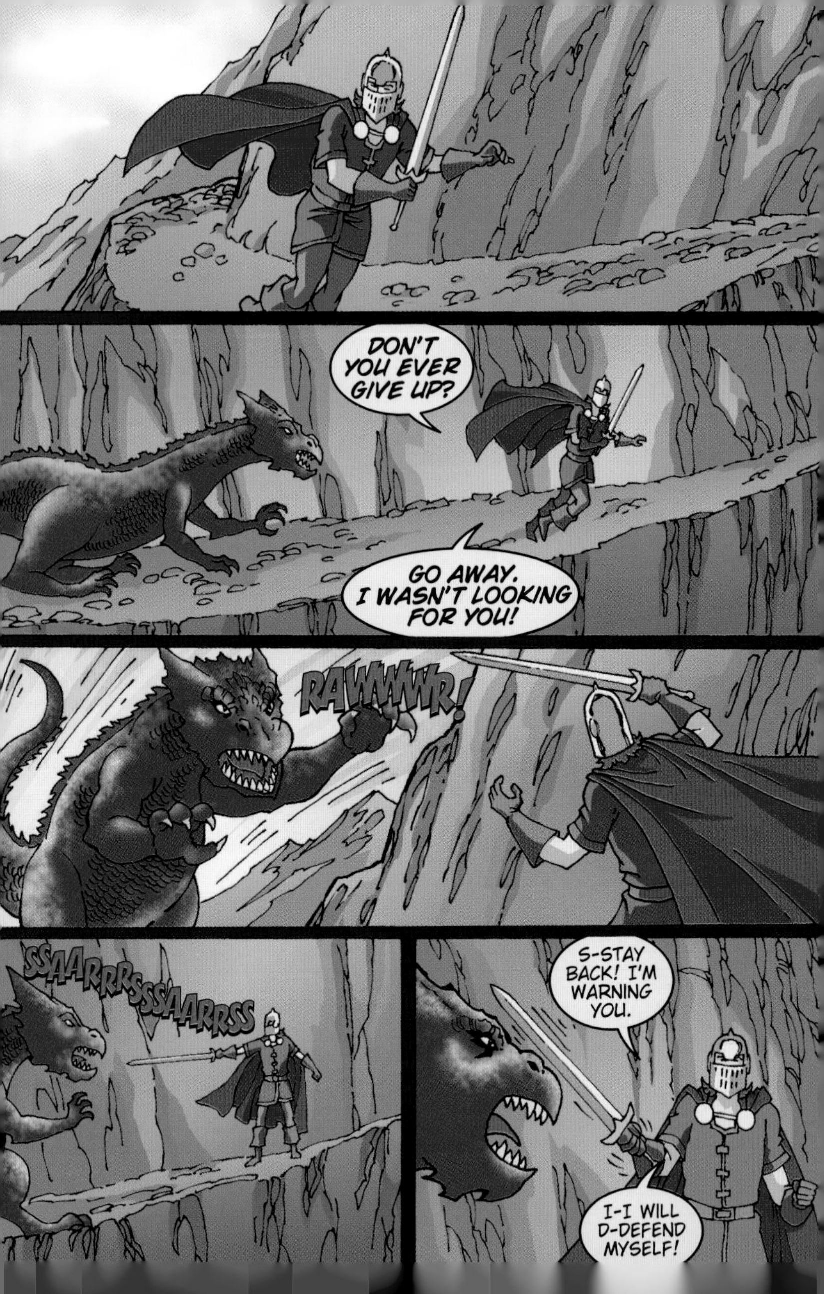
DON'T YOU EVER GIVE UP?
GO AWAY. I WASN'T LOOKING FOR YOU!
RAWWWR!
SSAARRRSSSAARRRSS
S-STAY BACK! I'M WARNING YOU.
I-I WILL D-DEFEND MYSELF!

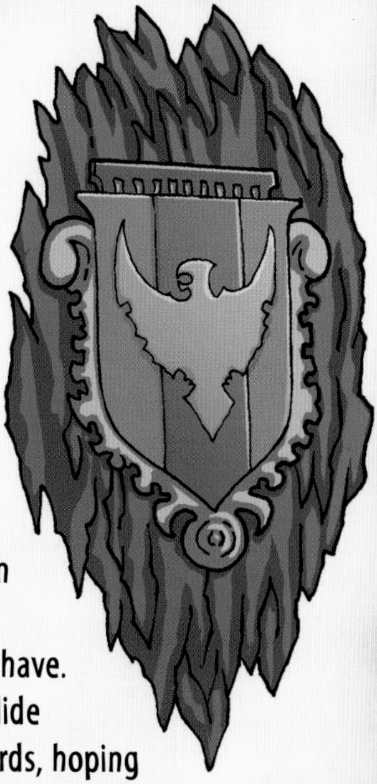

Your knees knock. What to do, what to do? Before you had somewhere to turn, somewhere to run, but coming up the mountain was a bad choice. You have no escape.

Your stomach gurgles, and it feels like a thousand butterflies are flitting about inside. Your mouth dries. Your teeth stick to the inside of your mouth. You run your tongue over them, wetting them with what little spittle you have.

Under your feet, loose stones slide about as you slide a step backwards, hoping to get a bit of balance. The beast watches you, its glistening eyes tracking your every movement. It almost seems to be waiting for you to slip before it strikes.

You reach out, and your hand brushes something smooth. You turn to see a small shield carved into the rock. The shield gives a bit when you press it.

GO ON TO THE NEXT PAGE.

The borkadrac roars and draws your attention. It's now or never. You spring forwards, pushing off your back foot. You land on your front foot and regain your balance. It's a risky move and Alaric would never commend you for it. Sloppy footwork, he would call it.

You push forwards with your sword arm, hoping to strike a point where the borkadrac is weak. You hear the delightful sound of the monster roaring.

The beast twists in pain, pulling your sword with it. You tug back, pulling the sword free and step backwards. Your ankle still hurts. You brace yourself against the mountain wall, keeping your sword ready.

You reach for the wall for balance and press the stone shield again. You know you're close to defeating this beast.

GO ON TO THE NEXT PAGE.

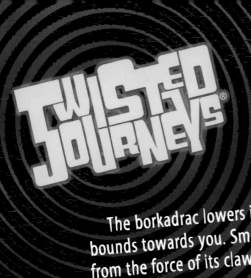

The borkadrac lowers its head and bounds towards you. Small rocks scatter from the force of its claws as it closes in.

WILL YOU...

...press the shield?
TURN TO PAGE 62.

...strike with your sword to defend yourself?
TURN TO PAGE 80.

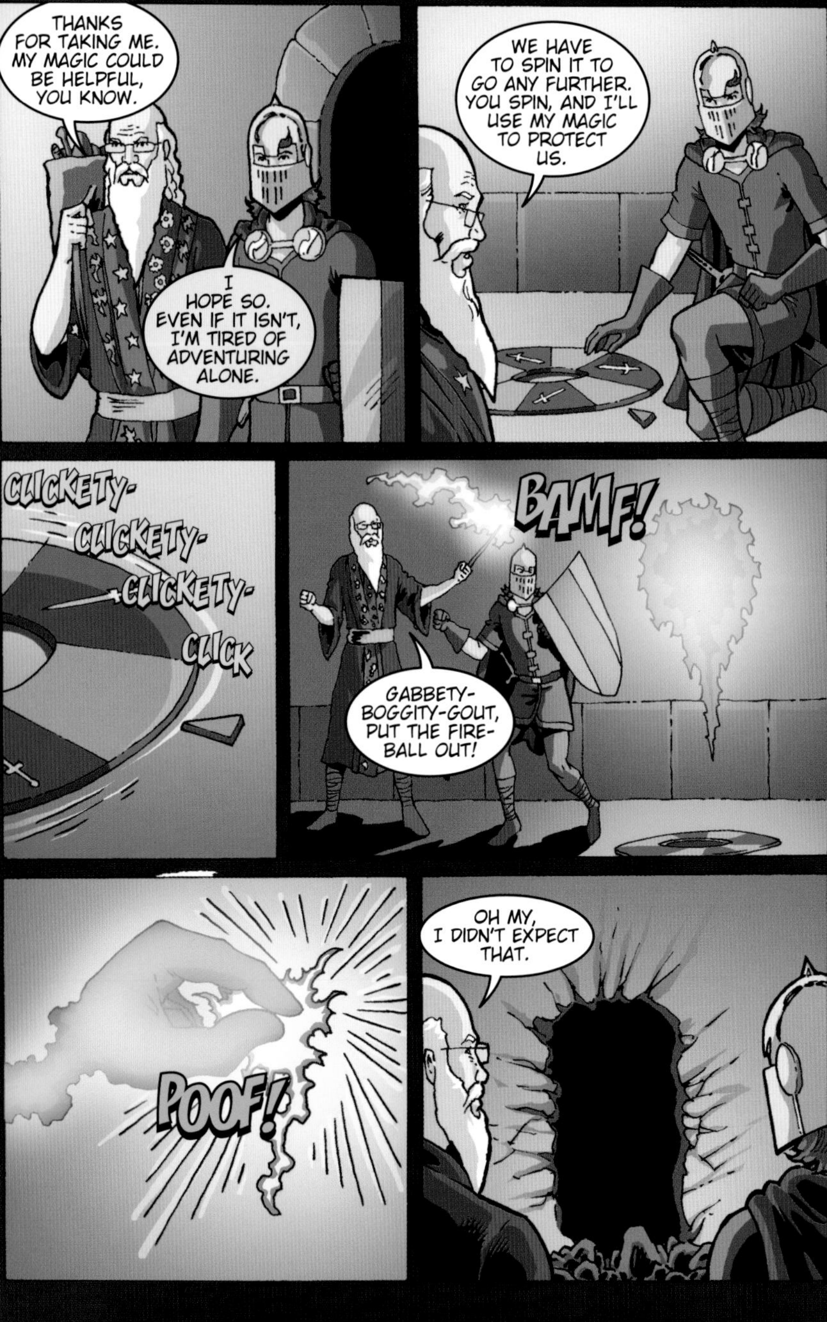
THANKS FOR TAKING ME. MY MAGIC COULD BE HELPFUL, YOU KNOW.
I HOPE SO. EVEN IF IT ISN'T, I'M TIRED OF ADVENTURING ALONE.
WE HAVE TO SPIN IT TO GO ANY FURTHER. YOU SPIN, AND I'LL USE MY MAGIC TO PROTECT US.
CLICKETY-
CLICKETY-
CLICKETY-
CLICK
BAMF!
GABBETY-BOGGITY-GOUT, PUT THE FIRE-BALL OUT!
POOF!
OH MY, I DIDN'T EXPECT THAT.

TURN TO PAGE 40.

You run back and grab Wizard Uchawi and pull him along with you, but the entrances to the room have disappeared. The walls show no trace that two doorways ever existed.

You look down at your boots and slump your shoulders. 'How long?'

Wizard Uchawi looks at you. He waits before he answers. 'Until the next hero comes along.'

'How long will that be?' You sit on a very large pillow. It's soft, and the velvet covering tickles your fingers.

'I waited over nine hundred years for you. It could easily be that long again.'

'Nine hundred years! I'll be dead.'

'No, not in here. You won't age a day.' Wizard Uchawi smiles. 'Do you play chess?'

'No, I don't know how.'

'Well, then, I'll teach you. You have all the time in the world to learn.'

THE END

You scramble hand over hand to the back of the hall. The glow of the fireball is immense and seems even hotter than before. Your skin stings from the heat, and you have to squint to protect your eyes.

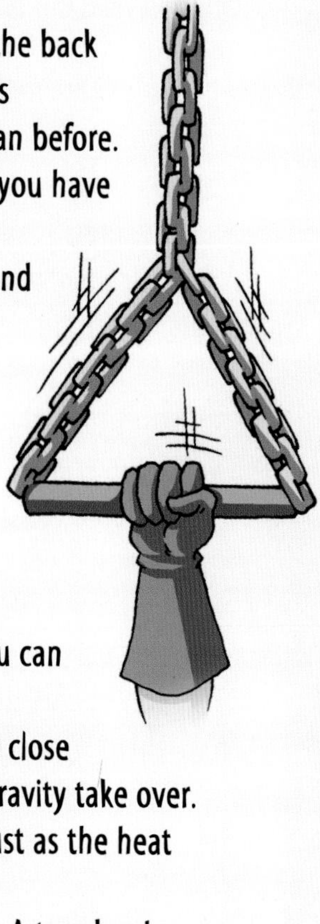

You pull yourself up to your feet and see a metal bar attached to a chain that runs to a pulley in the wall. The heat is getting worse. You know you won't make it if you stay here.

You stand up. The handle is just out of reach. So close…

The heat grows and you swear you can smell your hair as it singes.

You jump for the bar. Your fingers close around the cool metal and you let gravity take over.

The chain groans a bit but gives just as the heat becomes unbearable.

Below, the floor grinds and opens. A trapdoor!

GO ON TO THE NEXT PAGE.

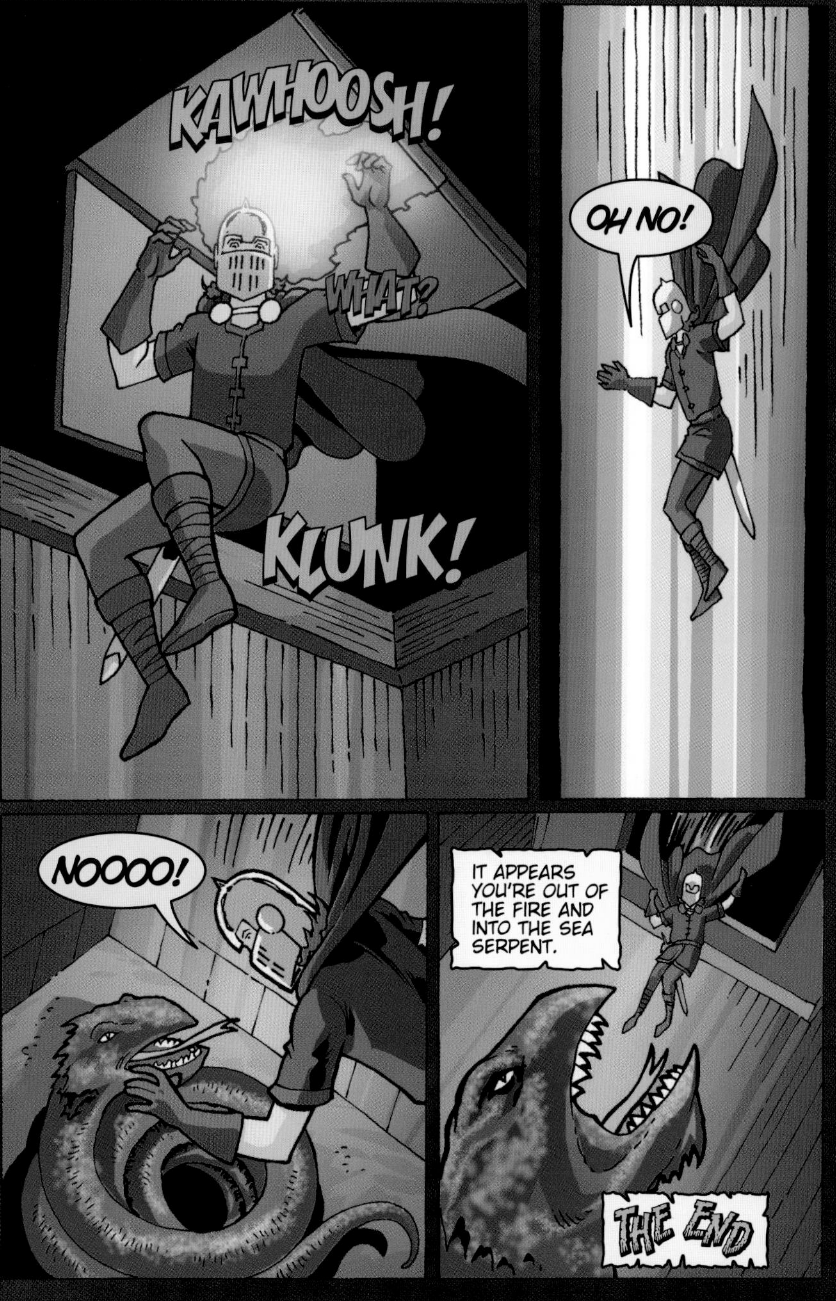
KAWHOOSH!
WHAT?
KLUNK!
OH NO!
NOOOO!
IT APPEARS YOU'RE OUT OF THE FIRE AND INTO THE SEA SERPENT.
THE END

Wizard Uchawi arches an eyebrow. 'You're braver than I thought.'

It's time to tighten the belt and head forwards. You look at Uchawi. 'Where does this go?'

The wizard rolls his eyes and throws his hands up. 'How should I know? I've been cooped up in a room for nine hundred years.'

Fine, you tell yourself. Obviously this hidden hallway must be important or it wouldn't be hidden, right? 'We go this way.' You take out your sword and grip your shield.

Wizard Uchawi softly harrumphs, 'This got me in trouble last time,' but he follows.

GO ON TO THE NEXT PAGE.

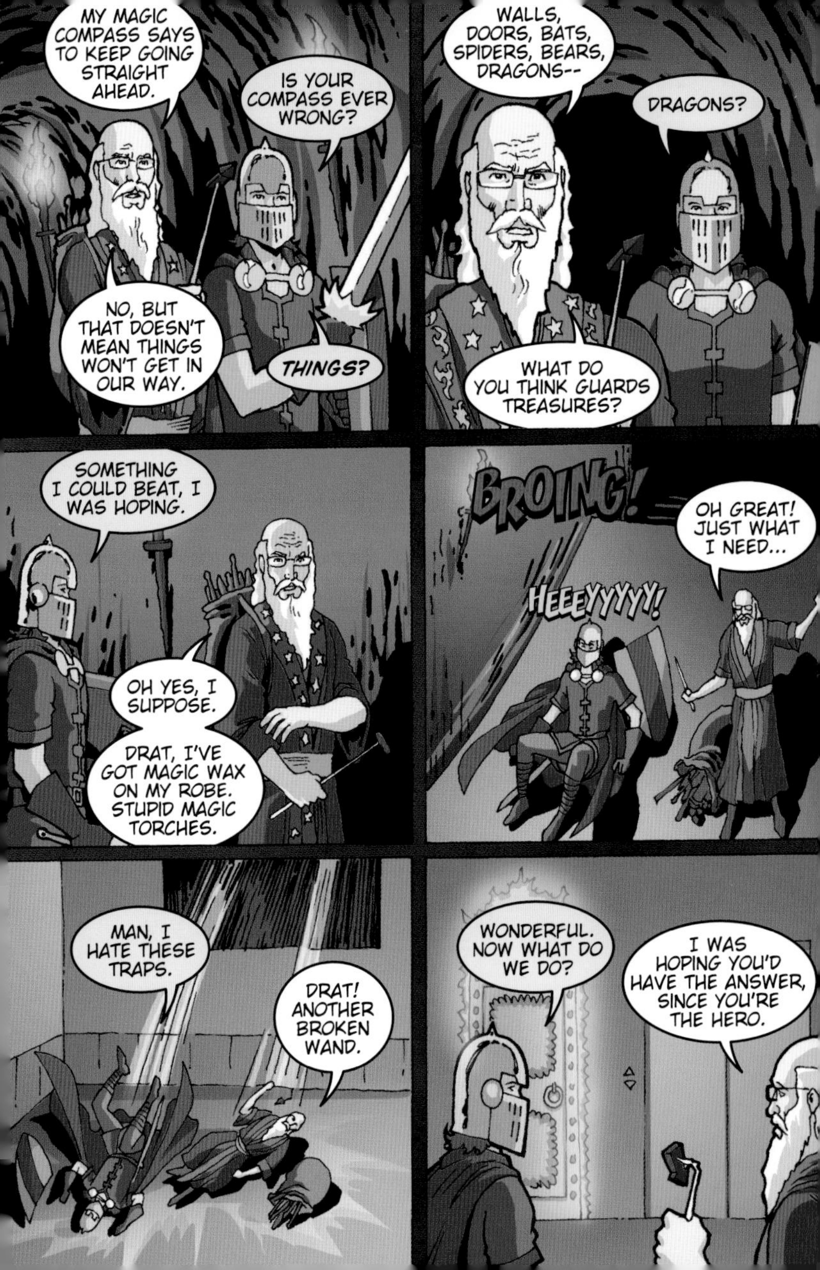

MY MAGIC COMPASS SAYS TO KEEP GOING STRAIGHT AHEAD.
IS YOUR COMPASS EVER WRONG?
NO, BUT THAT DOESN'T MEAN THINGS WON'T GET IN OUR WAY.
THINGS?
WALLS, DOORS, BATS, SPIDERS, BEARS, DRAGONS--
DRAGONS?
WHAT DO YOU THINK GUARDS TREASURES?
SOMETHING I COULD BEAT, I WAS HOPING.
OH YES, I SUPPOSE.
DRAT, I'VE GOT MAGIC WAX ON MY ROBE. STUPID MAGIC TORCHES.
BROING!
OH GREAT! JUST WHAT I NEED...
HEEEYYYYY!
MAN, I HATE THESE TRAPS.
DRAT! ANOTHER BROKEN WAND.
WONDERFUL. NOW WHAT DO WE DO?
I WAS HOPING YOU'D HAVE THE ANSWER, SINCE YOU'RE THE HERO.

No compass. Two doors. Three choices.

WILL YOU...

...press the up arrow?
TURN TO PAGE 48.

...press the down arrow?
TURN TO PAGE 88.

...open the glowing door?
TURN TO PAGE 110.

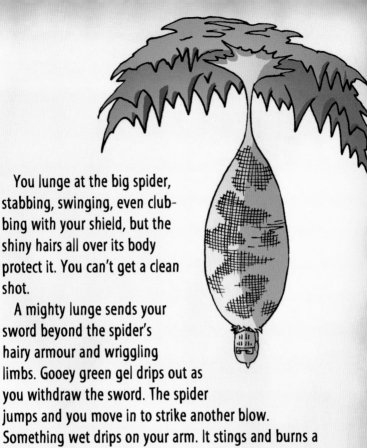

You lunge at the big spider, stabbing, swinging, even clubbing with your shield, but the shiny hairs all over its body protect it. You can't get a clean shot.

A mighty lunge sends your sword beyond the spider's hairy armour and wriggling limbs. Gooey green gel drips out as you withdraw the sword. The spider jumps and you move in to strike another blow. Something wet drips on your arm. It stings and burns a bit.

You swing your sword, but the spider dips out of the way and you feel a fang strike you on the back. The wound hurts for only a second. Then you can't feel your fingers — or anything else for that matter.

In moments, you are wrapped in spider silk. The spider drags you back to its lair, where it will keep you for a later day.

THE END

The glowing door leads to another one, which is covered with markings you don't understand and gems you've never seen. This has to be it. This has to be the treasure trove.

'I don't think that's where we want to go,' Wizard Uchawi says. He stands back and shakes his head. 'It looks awfully familiar.'

You open the door. Beyond you see gold coins piled high. Treasure chests overflow with pearl necklaces, gems and more. You want to say something, but words escape you.

'Don't go in there,' Wizard Uchawi says behind you.

You step into the room.

'It's just like – '

The door slams shut, cutting off Wizard Uchawi's words. The lights go dark, then flash back on.

The room is empty except for a sofa, a fountain and a table. You spin around. It looks just like the place where you found Wizard Uchawi.

The place where *you'll* be trapped for at least nine hundred years, too.

THE END

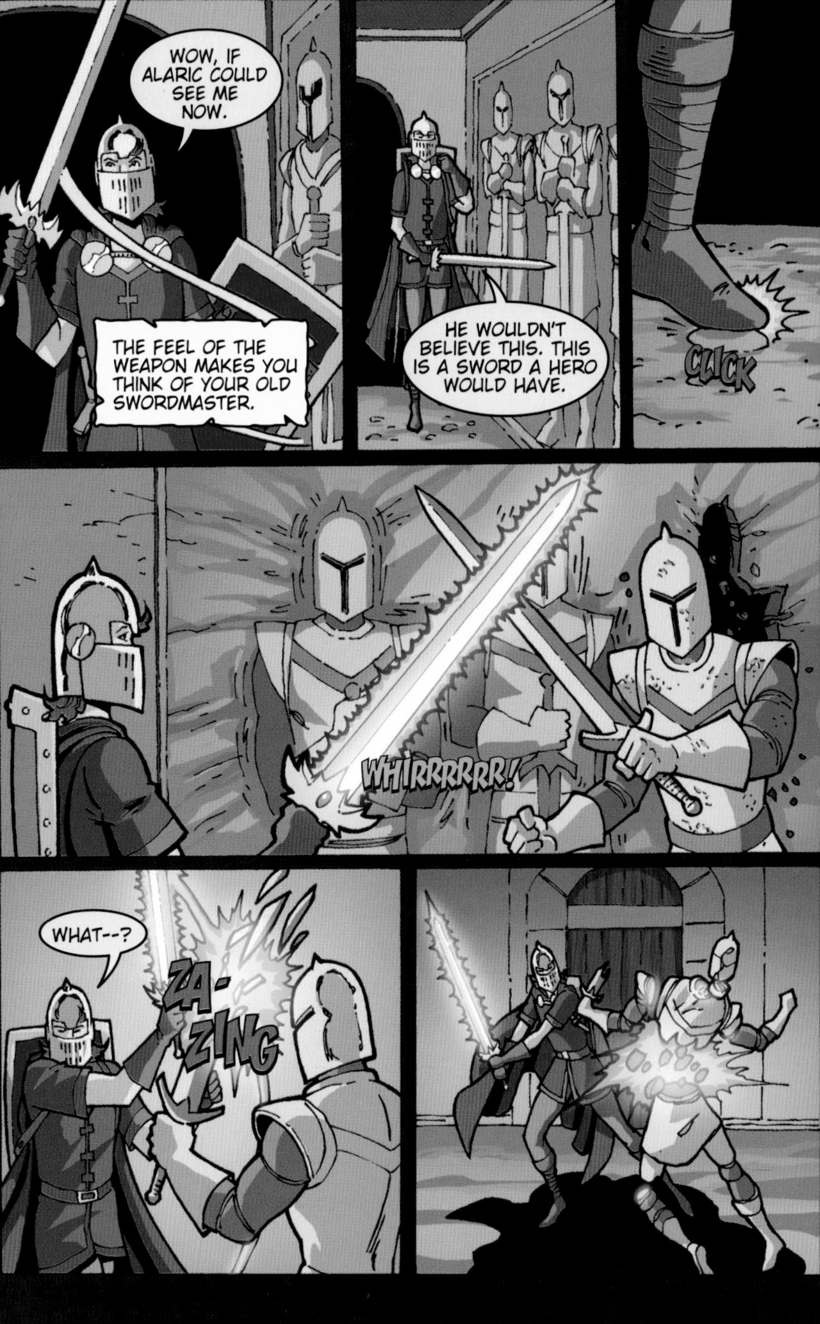
WOW, IF ALARIC COULD SEE ME NOW.
THE FEEL OF THE WEAPON MAKES YOU THINK OF YOUR OLD SWORDMASTER.
HE WOULDN'T BELIEVE THIS. THIS IS A SWORD A HERO WOULD HAVE.
CLICK
WHIRRRRRR!
WHAT--?
ZA-ZING

TURN TO PAGE 38.

READY FOR MORE ADVENTURES?

WHICH TWISTED JOURNEYS® WILL YOU TRY NEXT?

#1 CAPTURED BY PIRATES
Danger on the high seas! A band of scurvy pirates has boarded your ship. Can you keep them from turning you into shark bait?

#2 ESCAPE FROM PYRAMID X
You're on an archaeological mission to an ancient pyramid, complete with ancient mummies. Unfortunately for you, not everything that's ancient is also dead…

#3 TERROR IN GHOST MANSION
Halloween's not supposed to be this scary. You and your friends are trapped in a creepy old house with a family of ghosts. And they definitely aren't wearing costumes…

#4 THE TREASURE OF MOUNT FATE
Plenty of people have braved the monsters and magic of Mount Fate in search of its legendary treasure. But no one has ever lived to tell about their quest. Will you be the first?

This book was first published in the United States of America in 2007.

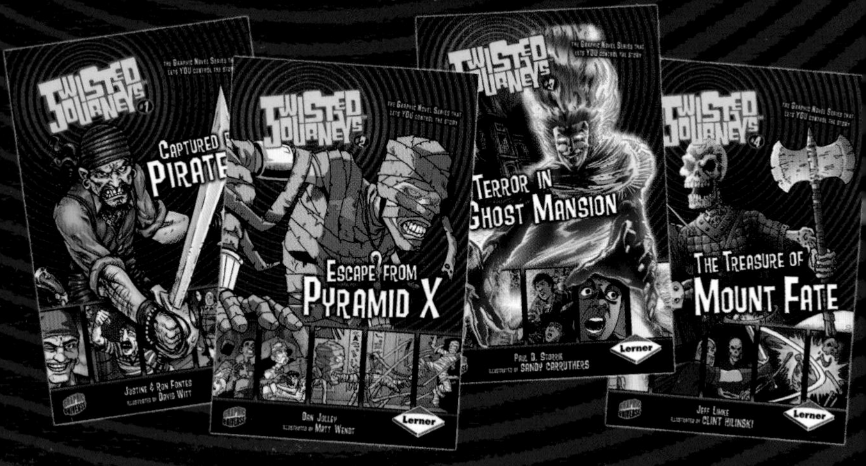
Twisted Journeys #1
Justine & Ron Fontes
David Witt
Twisted Journeys #2
Escape from Pyramid X
Dan Jolley
Matt Wendt
Lerner
Twisted Journeys #3
Terror in Ghost Mansion
Paul D. Storrie
Sandy Carruthers
Lerner
Twisted Journeys #4
The Treasure of Mount Fate
Jeff Limke
Clint Hilinski
Lerner